My JOURNEY WEST

APRIL 26, 2019
TO RICHARD
A NEW FRIEND

My
JOURNEY WEST

A pilot's lifetime in aviation

ALBERT ACKERMAN

Mill City Press
Minneapolis

Mill City Press, Inc.
322 First Avenue N, 5th floor
Minneapolis, MN 55401
612.455.2293
www.millcitypublishing.com

ISBN-13: 978-1-62652-534-4
LCCN: 2013920539

Book Design by Mary Kristin Ross

Printed in the United States of America

MILLCITY
PRESS

Introduction

This book chronicles how a passion for flying has shaped my life. Flying gave me a focus and a skill set that opened many doors, provided frequent opportunities to meet celebrities and politicians, and exposed me to more than a few life-threatening adventures. The events are more than enough for one lifetime.

People may ask: Was it because of my personality, my single-minded love for aviation, that drew people and adventures to me, or was it simply fate? This book will let you, the reader, decide.

Table of Contents

Chapter One
The Beginning

My story begins in 1950 during a summer vacation between my junior and senior years at Piedmont High in Piedmont, California. I got a job as a firefighter for the California Forestry Department, and my ranger station was in the foot-hills of the magnificent Sierra Nevada Mountains, close to the small town of Oroville, California. On my days off, I would drive my 1936 Hudson Terraplane to take in a movie, eat all the cheeseburgers available, and, of the utmost importance, chase girls. En route to and from town, I observed bright yellow J3 Piper Cubs flying in the area. I had always been entranced with airplanes and knew every type. I studied both allied and axis warplanes during World War II (WWII) and sketched them by the hour.

I decided to inquire about an airplane ride, since with my firefighter pay I had money to burn for the first time in my life. The local airport was not more than a grass strip with a WWII veteran aviator trying to eke out a living with some old, tired surplus aircraft. The Piper J3 ride cost three dollars. During the flight, the pilot asked if I would like to take over the controls. EUREKA!

My goal in life was decided in that moment. I was going to be a pilot. I returned on following days off, and the rides turned into impromptu flying lessons. I took to flying like a duck to water. In about three hours of instruction, a very short time by most standards, my ad-lib instructor cleared me to solo in that J3 Cub. I only realized years later what a significant day this was in my life. Summer vacation ended too quickly, no more flying. I returned home for my senior year of High School.

#1 PIPER J3 CUB

Those flying lessons and my three solo takeoffs and landings were in complete violation of 1950 era flying rules. I did not have a required student permit, and my new friend did not hold an instructor's license. Remember, this was 1950, when bending the rules just a "skoch" (small amount) was not uncommon. We were emerging from the war as a world power. Unfortunately, not long afterwards, America found itself involved in fighting an undeclared "limited war" in Korea, which was in reality a police action. Americans had to adjust to the realities of having become the world's policeman. But, back in the States, life was much simpler, and independent thinking and self-reliance were becoming prevalent. This transition for America was paid with the lives of thousands of American youth, some of whom were my high school buddies.

Looking back, the innocence of my youth had ended abruptly two years earlier, when I was fourteen years old. After the war, my father was a traveling salesman covering California and the Great Northwest. He would be gone weeks at a time. One day he returned home and announced he was leaving my mother and me and was gone the next day. He never sent a penny of support, and there were no bank savings to draw on. My mother was a full-time housewife without marketable skills, so the responsibility of man of the house fell squarely upon my shoulders.

Mom got a job as a sales clerk at the local five-and- dime store, and I found any weekend or part-time work I could. These meager wages did not come close to paying the monthly bills. My dear mother, who had never consumed a stronger drink than a champagne cocktail, turned to alcohol to ease her heartbreak. For many months, I was in fear of losing my remaining parent. We were headed for the poorhouse at a high rate of speed. There were no government welfare programs available in 1947.

My aunt, mother's oldest sister, and husband Herman Wobber, who made a fortune in the early motion picture industry and became a multi-millionaire, came to our rescue with monetary support. This family aid ended when I graduated from high school in 1951. I was expected to find a job, support myself, and help my mother. There was no extra money available, nor did my income qualify for any loans to continue flying lessons or attend college. I let an uneventful year pass, earning money as best I could through endless odd jobs. The local blood bank advertised to pay 20 dollars a pint for certain types of blood. My O-negative type qualified, putting dollars in my pocket, a lot of money to me at the time. I gave blood numerous times, helping to sustain me during this tough period of my life.

These uncertain days ended abruptly one evening in February of 1953. I received a telephone call from a friend's father who was on the Berkeley, California, draft board. He warned me that I was on the list to be drafted into the army next month. I had no desire to go to Korea as an infantryman. My fascination with airplanes made enlisting in the air force, thereby avoiding the draft, an easy decision. I had no inkling of what may lay ahead of me in the military, but I planned to serve my country to the best of my ability.

When I entered military service, my mother moved in with my aunt and uncle. On my first leave from the US Air Force on a visit to my mother, Uncle Herman pulled me aside and said, "We need to talk." He asked if I knew he had supported my mother and me over the last several years. I replied, "Yes, sir," and I told him how much it had meant to us. His next question: "When do you plan on paying me back?" Somewhat speechless, I blurted out, "Whenever I can, Uncle Herman."

He next inquired as to how much money I was making each month. As an airman basic, in my first month of duty, I earned 87 dollars per month. He immediately replied, "You and I will talk about this again in the future."

To a multi-millionaire, back when a million was a lot of money, 87 dollars a month must have stunned him into submission. As a survivor of the depression, Uncle Herman's rag-to-riches success story was built soundly on the foundation of hard work and penny pinching. As harsh as his inquiry regarding repayment may sound this many years removed from that reality, in context it was not unexpected or resented. He never brought up the subject again, and I always held him in the highest regard until his death in 1965 at the age of 86.

My air force commitment was for a period of four years. A minimum of two years of college was required to apply for aviation cadets. During the third week of basic training, an officer came to my barracks one evening and called out my name. He told me as a result of my air force aptitude testing scores, I qualified to take the aviation cadet entrance examinations. I never expected to be considered for such an opportunity, not meeting the college requirements. So I have always looked back at this as a backdoor entry to the cadet program.

I thought the entrance exams would be a waste of time until I noted the start of cadet testing was the same day I was scheduled for "KP" (Kitchen Police) duty. I had already endured KP duty once, and the aviation cadet testing now became my focus. I took the testing with the mindset that I would do my very best, but I did not have expectations of success.

After four days of medical exams, aptitude testing on a range of subject matter, and coordination exercises, we were called to base theatre where an officer stated, "If your name is called out, you have failed to qualify and should leave the building." Every time he prepared to read out a name, I slid to the edge of my seat, ready to stand up and depart. From the best of my memory, only eight of the original 50 plus candidates remained seated when he closed the book of names and stated to us, "Congratulations, gentlemen. You are among the select few that have qualified to become aviation cadets." I sat glued to my seat, not daring to move, fearful he had somehow missed reading out my name.

It took several weeks for the reality to sink in, and my feet seemed to never touch the ground as I walked back to my barracks. My drill sergeant had already been notified of my acceptance into the program. It was amazing how his attitude toward me changed. No more KP or other crappy details for this airman. Perhaps he was afraid I would become his superior officer one day. For the first time in my life, I had a sense of superiority and destiny.

Orders arrived the following week for transfer to Lackland Air Force Base in San Antonio, Texas, for aviation cadet preflight training. This was my first foray outside of the great state of California, and I was not aware Texas was in the midst of the infamous seven-year drought that started in 1950 and lasted until 1957.

I was not prepared for the irrepressible heat, humidity, and frequent dust storms that were the norm in this forsaken part of the world. This was such a change from the typical seventy degree weather back in northern California. I stepped off the military transport train near the air base at 11:00 a.m. to an ambient temperature of 87 degrees. I had worn my air force wool dress blues from home. I would not make this kind of wardrobe error again. We spent over an hour in formation as the training officer welcomed us as the "privileged few" chosen for flight training. I thought I was going to pass out, and thought to myself, *this must be hell!*

Preflight was referred to as the "Tiger Program." The program was based on 24 hours of hazing by the upper class cadets, similar to what cadets experienced at US military academies. The purpose was to test our ability to perform under constant pressure so that we would not fail to prevail in wartime aerial combat.

An upperclassman from Pittsburgh, Pennsylvania, developed an intense disliking for me and took hazing to a new level every waking hour of the day. Although I can no longer remember his name, his face is firmly etched in my memory, and if I should happen to cross paths with him today, I would be tempted to kill the bastard.

Every cadet had to recite a comical quote when requested by an upperclassman. My choice was: "We are installing wheels on houses of ill repute." When asked why, I would respond with: "because we're hauling ass tonight!" Such was the time of my life.

Cadets were required to eat "square meals." The term came from British military lore where the dinner plate was a square piece of wood with a bowl that had been carved out to hold a serving of perpetual stew that was always cooking over a fire. A "square" was taken when traveling in hope of finding such a meal. Sailors used to eat off flat wooden boards that were square in shape and were usually not filled with food. However, after a difficult watch, they were given a large meal that filled the board, thus becoming a square meal.

During our training, we were required to sit formally at all meals, bolt upright, knees held firmly together, with arms at right-angles, so forming a square shape. Today, square meals have more to do with nutrition than the physical act of consumption.

A cadet standing in early morning formation was assessed "gigs" when the training officer took exception to uniform infractions involving alignment of the shirt, belt buckle, and trouser fly. A cadet was required to have these items in a perfect straight line at all times. Upperclassmen loved to yank a cadet's uniform shirt out of his pants just as he was running for an inspection, leaving him subject to receiving a "gig line" violation while standing for review. Gigs were also assessed for Saturday morning white-glove inspections, square meals infractions, and a host of other violations that were observed.

Upperclassmen made a point of watching the water

fountain very closely. They seemed to love to sneak up behind a new cadet and push the button before he could take a drink. The cadet was required to salute before the flow of water touched the basin. Those who moved too slowly were denied the opportunity to take a drink.

A cadet receiving excess weekly gigs was not allowed an open post, which meant off base on the weekends, and had to march off the gigs in full dress khaki uniform in an open field under the heat of the Texas sun. As you might imagine, gigs were avoided at all costs.

As an underclassman, I was constantly subjected to redress by upperclassmen. A typical encounter would go something like this: "Mister, hit a brace!" A brace was simply the act of coming to attention in the stiffest form attainable with back rigid and chin tucked into one's chest. The next demand was to quote the correct time. The required answer was as follows: "Sir, since the inner workings and hidden mechanisms of my chronometer are not in accordance with the great celestial movement by which time is commonly reckoned, I cannot safely state the correct time. Without fear of being too far wrong, sir, the correct time is . . ." Although most of the other required quotations now elude me, after almost sixty years, I can still recall the proper response to a request for time.

Unfortunately, several of my fellow cadets broke down under this intense pressure and took their own lives. One young man bled to death during the middle of the night after slashing his wrists in the shower room; another went absent without leave (AWOL) and stood by the railroad tracks near the base and stepped in front of a moving locomotive. As this was not bad enough, the worst death occurred when yet another cadet left the base without permission. He had checked himself into a flea-bag hotel in downtown San Antonio and swallowed rat poison. He was found and returned to the base hospital, but the medical staff was not able to save him.

My twenty years of life had not prepared me for this experience. Today's military might take another approach, but it was a different day and time during a war, and the program moved on with little or no change in intensity. There was no time to look backward in this pressure cooker environment.

I have always wondered why these young fellow cadets chose to end their lives. Perhaps they had led too sheltered lives, with no setbacks or crises to deal with. Being cast into this new, chaotic environment with no relief in sight except resigning, and facing a difficult return home with the stigma of having failed, perhaps for these somewhat naïve gentlemen, the situation was all too overwhelming. I felt so privileged to be there, any thoughts of physical harm to myself or going AWOL never remotely entered my mind. I was committed to endure the worst preflight had to offer.

After surviving the three months of hell known as cadet preflight, I arrived in Bainbridge, Georgia, for primary flight training. It was a civilian operated flight school under contract with the air force. The program was for 20 hours of instruction. The trainer used was a Piper PA-18 Super Cub, which turned out to be a souped-up version of the little bright yellow J3 Cub I had soloed in the years before. The trainer had an engine developing twice the horsepower, but with the same flight characteristics as the J3. With all that extra power, I thought I'd gone to heaven in a rocket ship on my first takeoff.

#2 PIPER PA 18 USAF BASIC TRAINER 1953

Those who survived this initial training moved on to more advanced airplanes at other bases. The advanced trainers were the North American T6 (Texan) powered by a Pratt & Whitney 600 horsepower radial engine and the T28 (Trojan) powered by a Curtiss-Wright 800 horsepower radial engine. Today both of these planes are still being flown by civilian owners.

My instructor thought I was a whiz kid and frequently asked, "Cadet Ackerman, have you ever flown before?" I always emphatically denied that I had. I completed about ten hours of flight training when the Korean War ended in July 1953. Unfortunately, I was caught up in the Officer and Cadet Reduction in Force (RIF) process. A reduction in manpower was just the military's way of eliminating too many officers and too many cadets without a war to justify their expense.

A history of a twice broken wrist and an x-ray showing a small fracture line was all the military required to wash me out of the cadet program. What a disappointment, as I had planned to be the best fighter pilot in the USAF.

Since I had enlisted, washing out of cadets did not mean discharge from the air force. I still had a three-and-a-half-year commitment to fulfill. After months of basically accomplishing nothing on so called "casual status," I had the good fortune to be transferred back to Parks AFB in Livermore, California, where I had attended basic training and qualified for aviation cadets. Definite feelings of déejà vu and a return back to my home state surrounded me.

With my cadet background, I was assigned to work in the instrument simulator training department. My boss was Master Sergeant Luman H. Hicks, a survivor of World War II. He was a glider pilot on D-Day, June 6, 1944. The casualty rate for glider pilots on that day was horrendous. Out of 515 gliders launched, 97 percent were damaged beyond repair either on landing or by enemy fire and being abandoned in the field. Sergeant Hicks never talked much about D- Day. I'm sure his recollections of that day were too painful to deliberate.

Sergeant Hicks turned out to be a blessing in my life and I shall never forget him. He soon learned of my desire to be a pilot. Besides receiving many hours of instrument simulator time, which I could never have afforded in a civilian school, on most duty days, he would always tell me after noon chow to get off base and he would cover for the rest of the day. I started hanging around the local civilian airport, Buchanan Field in the town of Concord. I met and became friends with the owner of Pacific States Aviation. It was a small flight school and charter company struggling to grow in hard times. He gave me any and all odd jobs to perform in trade for an hour of flying time. I fueled, cleaned, parked, and tied down the company planes and helped the mechanic with repairs.

My duties also included a weekly scrubbing of the restrooms. As my new boss gained confidence in my work, he let me manage the company in the late daylight hours during the summer months. This gave him some well-deserved time off and earned me extra flight hours.

By the time of my honorable discharge from the air force in March 1957, I had earned my private, commercial, and flight instructor ratings. These ratings became my gateway to numerous other opportunities in aviation in the years ahead of me.

Chapter Two
Flight Instructor

It was back to civilian life and an offer from Pacific States Aviation for a full-time job as a charter pilot and flight instructor. I still had a military commitment for the next six years to be on a 48-hour callback to active duty due to my critical air force specialty as an instrument simulator instructor. Fortunately, this recall never occurred. By the end of 1958, I had added instrument and multi-engine ratings to my pilot certificate. Now my main focus was to build my flying hours.

One of the more humorous events of flight instruction occurred when a student on a solo cross-country trip ran out of gas and made a forced landing in a lettuce field by Salinas, California. My assignment was to take some gas and retrieve the airplane. The soil conditions were quite soft, causing the tires to dig in, and several takeoff attempts failed. By now, there was lettuce strewn everywhere from the prop wash (pilot jargon for the wind created behind a turning propeller).

As I positioned for another takeoff try, a pickup truck arrived at the edge of the field with a very unhappy farmer, who appeared to be brandishing a shotgun. That quickly gave the airplane and me the necessary incentive to get the hell out of there. I did manage to coax my flying machine into the air on the verge of a stall, looking back at enough airborne lettuce to make a gigantic Caesar salad and a farmer shaking his angry fist in my direction.

I hunkered down back at home base, waiting for a call

from the Federal Aviation Authority (FAA). Thankfully, that call never came. The poor lettuce farmer, in his frustration, probably never noted the aircraft registration number. None of us were well off enough to offer any kind of restitution. I hope my foray didn't raise the price of a head of lettuce a penny or two.

A well-known local physician arrived one day and stated he was interested in flying lessons and asked for an introductory flight. Our trainer airplane was an Aeronca model 7AC Champion, simply nicknamed "the Champ." It was manufactured by the Aeronca Aircraft Company of Middletown, Ohio, and first flew in 1944. The airframe was built of welded steel tubing, covered with Irish linen fabric and had two seats in tandem. It was powered by a Continental, opposed four-cylinder engine, producing 65 horsepower, with a fixed two-bladed propeller. Over 10,000 Champs were delivered before production ceased in 1951. I gave Doc a preflight briefing and

#3 AERONCA 7AC CHAMPION

strapped him in the front seat, the normal position in a Champ for both passengers and students. The engine run-up and all preflight checks were normal. Upon reaching about two hundred feet of altitude after takeoff, the engine, without warning, abruptly quit. This was much too low to attempt a turn back to the airport. I lowered the nose to maintain airspeed and looked ahead for a safe emergency landing spot. As soon as I lowered the nose, the engine came back to life, and I was able to gain a few feet of altitude before the engine would quit again. I slowly made a turn back to the runway, gaining a few precious feet of altitude each time the engine stopped, and ran with every raising and lowering of the nose.

The Champ had no electrical system, so communication was done by hollering above the cabin noise. I kept hollering to Doc up front, "Don't panic! We will be okay!" He never uttered a word while keeping a death grip with both hands on the tubular structure that supported the windshield and staring straight ahead at what I'm sure he thought would be a spot on the ground where he would take his last breath.

I was able to make a safe landing and clear the runway. I exited the plane, asking the doc to stay seated while I looked around the engine cowling, trying to determine our problem. There was no evidence of an oil leak or any other indications of a major engine failure. I then decided to check the fuel level. The second I removed the fuel cap and heard a rush of air enter the tank; I knew what had caused our engine stoppage. The Champ had a gravity feed fuel system with a vented fuel cap that allowed air to replace the vacated space in the tank as fuel was consumed. Without a vented cap, a vacuum would build in the tank, disrupting the fuel supply to the engine. Someone had put an unvented cap on our Champ! A vented fuel cap was an item I would never again miss checking on an Aeronca Champ preflight inspection.

I turned back to the doc to tell him that I had found out what the problem was, and as soon as I could replace the cap, we could continue our flight. He was no longer in his front seat or around the plane. I looked up to observe a cloud of dust as his car made a rapid exit from the parking lot. I was somewhat dismayed the doctor didn't have time to say goodbye or at least thank me for a safe return to the ground.

Another student got lost and landed at Palmdale AFB, the home of the famous Lockheed Skunkworks, one of the most restricted military sites in the United States. Again, my job was to retrieve the plane, make explanations and apologies to the base commander, and fill out the reams of paperwork required to release the airplane. As I climbed into the airplane to depart, the base commander bid me a fond farewell and a firm order: "Please do not ever come back!"

At times a cross-country flight can result in embarrassing consequences. In 1957, Pacific States Aviation purchased a new Aeronca Champ trainer. The Champion factory was located in Osceola, Wisconsin. The newest Champ had been designed with a tricycle landing gear, instead of the standard tail wheel configuration, and was called the Tri-Champ. The tricycle gear made much easier takeoff and landings for student pilots. However, the additional drag of the nose wheel reduced the cruising speed to a paltry 90 miles per hour.

I was given the job to fly the new trainer home, a distance of 1,575 air miles. I flew to Minneapolis on a Western Airlines (long defunct) DC-6 and then took

#4 AERONCA TRI-CHAMP

the train to Osceola. This was a grand adventure for a gung ho 24-year-old pilot.

I got a late start from the factory. With unfamiliar terrain and too much sightseeing, I actually got lost for the first time in my early flying days. I managed to find Sioux Falls, South Dakota, as darkness was falling. After a restless night, with a somewhat deflated ego, I arose at the crack of dawn and ate a hearty breakfast at a local "greasy spoon," knowing this would be my only meal for the day. Determined not to get lost again, I departed with the sun rising behind me, anticipating a wonderful day flying over the Heartland of America and soaking in countryside I had never seen before.

About thirty minutes into the flight, a low-lying fog formed, completely obscuring the ground. About the same time the first discomforting signs of stomach cramps, and need to find a restroom, arrived. I desperately looked for a hole in the overcast below, to land anywhere, a road, a field, ANYWHERE! To my dismay, as far as I could see in every direction, the fog layer was rock solid.

The cramps and the need grew, and I recalled the eggs eaten at breakfast in Sioux Falls had a strange flavor. The bastards had served me rancid eggs! I tried to relieve myself through the sliding cockpit side window, which proved impossible while trying to fly the plane at the same time. The cramps were now unbearable and I came close to passing out. I had no choice but to relieve myself. What would the boss say when his new light blue upholstered seat arrived home with some tinges of brown? I unfolded some aeronautical charts, placed them on the seat, and did the unthinkable.

I flew on over an hour in this horrendous condition. The ground fog started to dissipate, and the town of Alliance, Nebraska, appeared just ahead. A small town with a small airport, where I prayed no one would be in attendance. I taxied up to the only building on the field, and who walks out but a woman. I was tempted to taxi back to the runway and takeoff, but lack of fuel, plus my deplorable condition, dictated otherwise.

I reluctantly exited the plane and warned the lady to stay back. I think she had already caught a whiff of the aroma drifting into the air from the Tri-Champ and a totally humiliated pilot. This lady turned out to be one the kindest persons I have ever met, and she reminded me that airplane people are the greatest. She directed me to a washroom, and then drove herself to town.

She purchased cleaning supplies and a new pair of underwear and pants in my correct size. She insisted on helping me clean the plane, and, to our amazement, after hours of hard work, the light blue seat and the rest of the cockpit looked almost new. Needless to say those aeronautical charts that somewhat saved the day were history. I still imagined the faint odor of rotten eggs for the remainder of the trip.

The rest of this arduous journey, over 31 flying hours, went without any more disasters and minimum weather delays. Crossing both the Rocky and Sierra Nevada Mountains proved quite challenging in the Tri-Champ, but I overcame with superb pilot skill and daring (couldn't resist that).

Although my travel allowances were always austere, limiting my choices, I definitely did a better job of restaurant selection for the remaining overnight stops.

My childhood and lifelong friend, Pete McCoy, came out for a ride after I obtained my pilot and instructor licenses and was immediately bit by the flying bug. I gave him numerous hours of flight instruction, and, with the input of other instructors, he earned his private pilot certificate. We had many wonderful hours of flying together while impressing the lady friends of the day. Pete still has his original logbook from the 1950s with entries of my signature signing off an hour of flight instruction. I have lost too many lifelong friends over the past several years. Pete and I are survivors, and even though living 1,000 miles apart, we are in constant contact with one another. These are the times and memories that grow ever more precious with each passing year.

The most rewarding days of instructing were teaching a paraplegic to fly and then clearing him to take his first solo flight. The airplane used for this training was an Ercoupe, two passengers side-by-side seating, powered by a Continental, opposed four cylinder 85 horsepower engine.

The Ercoupe was produced in the United States shortly after the end of World War II by the Engineering and Research Corporation (ERCO) out of Riverdale, Maryland. This plane was designed with interconnected controls, eliminating the need for rudder pedals. The only pedal on the floor was for braking, which he could operate with a specially modified cane.

The first couple of lessons went poorly, and I was tempted, but didn't have the heart, to tell him I didn't think this was working out. In ensuing flights his confidence grew, he became more relaxed,

#5 ERCOUPE MODEL 415G

and I had the pleasure of teaching him to fly. Solo day arrived, and I stood at the edge of the runway observing his takeoffs and landings with some apprehension. He did a good job, and after completing his last landing, he taxied over to pick me up with tears streaming down his face. I reached into the cockpit to shake his hand and found a tear or two running down my face, a moment not soon forgotten.

Ercoupe and other manufacturers of small aircraft at the end of WWII had the idea with all the military pilots returning many would want to continue flying. This business theory turned out to be sadly incorrect. Small plane production languished for the reminder of the forties and well into the fifties. By then Ercoupe and several other small plane manufacturers were bankrupt. Business leaders were perplexed as to why the expected boom in personal aviation did not materialize. I suspect, however, those who endured the austerity of military aviation and the rigors of flying an airplane while dodging bullets during wartime opted to put that part of their résumé behind them.

Many of my students were Korean Vets using their GI bill for flight training. A few were serious about making aviation a career. To the rest, it was just as a paid for adventure. These students made instructing very frustrating and I ran a couple off. That nearly got me run off by the boss, complaining I was costing him money. My comeback: "Better to lose some money than wreck one of your planes!" I guess I never developed an understanding for those who would not do anything to experience the joy of flight.

Flight instructing was one way of building flight hours to qualify for the airlines or a corporate flying position. After a time, instructing became tedious. Every new student was no longer a challenge but a boring repetition. I longed and dreamed that a real flying job would come my way.

Chapter Three
Chartering

Our top-of-the-line charter plane was an 1956 Cessna 172. The plane had a high-wing design, accommodated four passengers and had a fixed landing gear. It was powered by an opposed six cylinder Continental 145 horsepower engine, with a whopping top cruising speed of 125 miles per hour.

Instrumentation was very basic, especially for instrument flying. She was equipped with an altimeter, airspeed and vertical speed indicators, an electric driven needle-ball, which provided basic roll and yaw

#6 1956 CESSNA 172

information, but no pitch information. A Venturi-driven attitude gyro provided both roll and pitch information, which would not erect (function) until an airspeed of 80 miles per hour was reached. It also had one radio, a Narco Super Homer, a vacuum tube radio of the era with 10 fixed transmitting frequencies and a receiver with a tuning knob, which resembled the handle of the old time coffee grinders.

#7 NARCO SUPER HOMER

Several charter customers used our services to make airline connections at San Francisco International Airport (SFO), which was a short thirty-minute flight from Buchanan Field. Most of these flights were scheduled in the early morning hours when the fog in the Bay Area was so thick you could cut it with a knife. There was no control tower at the field then, so no flight plan was filed.

I would taxi into position for takeoff with only three to four runway lights in view down the runway due to the thick fog. I only had reference to the needle-ball and airspeed in climbing through the fog, before reaching clear skies at about an altitude of 1,500 feet.

By this time, my Venturi-driven attitude gyro would be functioning, providing me with both roll and pitch information for use on my instrument landing system (ILS) approach to SFO. The ILS system of the day sent out two electronic beams. One was called the Localizer (LOC), which kept you on the center line of the runway; the other was called the Glide Slope (GS), which kept you at the correct descending altitudes to reach the threshold of the runway at 200 feet.

My little Narco Super Homer could receive the LOC but not the GS. I would circle above the clouds in the clear, watching airliners of the day (DC-6s, DC-7s, and Lockheed Constellations) shooting the ILS approach. I made a note of where they entered the top of the fog layer, knowing they were established on the GS. I calculated that was the spot where I could intercept my imaginary GS. I would receive an approach clearance, get centered on the LOC, and head for that magic spot. Upon entering the clouds, I would deploy 20 degrees of flap, set up 400-feet-per-minute decent, and watch for the runway approach lights to appear through the overcast, guiding me to the runway threshold.

I shot many ILS approaches at SFO using this technique, several down to ILS minimums: 200 feet and one half mile visibility. I would then have to cool my heels at SFO until around noon when the fog would dissipate so I could return home, as there was no instrument approach back at Buchanan Field.

Those flights probably broke almost every rule in the Federal Aviation Administration book of regulations. I was twenty-three years old, completely bullet proof and confident I could do anything with an airplane without bending it or injuring myself. I look back at those days and say to myself, "Bullet proof my ass. I was just plain stupid!."

The Contra Costa County Sheriff Department contracted the company to transport prisoners, so I was deputized as a Deputy Sheriff. The aircraft used was a Cessna 195 powered by a 300 horsepower Jacobs Radial Engine, nicknamed "the Jake." The prisoners we hauled were not hardened criminals, mostly petty thieves; behind on alimony or child support payments, etc. A real deputy would always accompany me. Two prisoners were handcuffed and placed in the back seat, and we cruised home with that old Jake engine purring along with a confidence-building soft rumble.

The deputy would "wink" in my direction and give me a nudge. This was my signal to slowly lean the fuel mixture until that purring engine would start complaining by vibrating, backfiring, and seeming to be on the verge of failure. All you could see from the back seat were four gigantic white eyes and the question, "Mista Sheriff, is we

#8 CESSNA 195

gonna fall?" It seemed my job was always to clean up those wet spots on the backseats.

Several funeral homes contracted us to deliver corpses. I do not know if body bags in use today were available in those days or whether the undertakers could not afford them. My bodies were always loosely wrapped in a sheet and placed in the copilot seat next to me, making wonderful company. On a hot day, opening the cockpit air vents would cause the covering sheet to partly blow open, making the remaining flight a bit gruesome. The change in altitude and pressure would cause some corpses to expel air, sounding like a groan or whistle. The first time that happened, I literally wet my pants. One thing, those folks never complained about being too hot or cold, and not once commented, "That was a bumpy ride. I'm sure glad to be on the ground again!"

Another charter trip in that ol' Cessna 172 was with a local family on vacation that had a car accident in Ely,

Nevada, seriously injuring the wife. Getting her home by ground transportation was not practical, so we became an air ambulance service. The back seats of the Cessna were removed to accommodate a litter, and her daughter accompanied me. During the flight, she made several comments that hinted of being amorous. I behaved myself as; after all, she was a paying customer. We arrived at Ely late in the afternoon and scheduled a next morning departure. The ambulance pulled up and unloaded a large woman that, counting her luggage and the litter, weighed close to 300 pounds. I elected to take off with some concern about being over the aircraft's safe weight for the departure. The hospital had fed her a generous breakfast that morning, which in about 30 minutes into the flight, decorated the back of the airplane.

Reno was my first fuel stop, and by this time, thankfully, the poor lady had no more breakfast to give. I explained to the daughter that she and her luggage would have to stay in Reno. With her aboard, we would be too heavy to climb to a safe altitude crossing the Sierra Nevada Mountains. She understood and said she would find her way home. The last leg over the mountains was quite bumpy, and I was thankful I had made sure my passenger didn't have any lunch in Reno.

We arrived to waiting family and friends, and she could not stop thanking me for getting her home safely. As fate would have it, several days later, a company Cessna 140 had engine problems in Reno. When the aircraft was repaired, I was flown to Reno to bring it home. As I was fueling the plane, the daughter that I had left behind walked up. She had been unable to get a ride home and asked if I could take her. I replied, "No problem. I would enjoy your company".

Before I continue with this story, I must explain a Cessna 140 is very small two-passenger tail wheel plane powered by a 90 horsepower engine with a top cruising speed of 110 miles per hour. Side-by-side seating in a cabin width of just 42 inches made it very cozy for two.

#9 1948 CESSNA 140

In these austere times, I was always bound by a very limited expense account. Staying overnight in Reno would have been the safe and smart plan. Having only a grand total of three dollars and change in my pocket, after paying for fuel, left sleeping in the airplane my only option, no thanks to a cold cramped night in that 42-inch wide cabin. So a late departure at dusk meant crossing over the mountains would be in the dark. Crossing the Sierra Nevada Mountains at night in a Cessna 140 is not for the faint of heart. I do not know for what reasons, maybe doubt that I and our little puddle jumper were up to the task, but about halfway across the mountains, she came on me with unbridled passion. It was almost impossible to keep my flying machine right-side up while trying to manipulate the controls, amongst her embraces, in that tiny cockpit.

Due to the very limited space, along with a mechanical flap actuator handle located between the two seats, made going all the way totally impossible. I was on course and had the distant lights of Sacramento, the state capitol, in sight when she began to passionately embrace me again. I would look up and discover we had turned 180 degrees and were headed back to Reno. After this happened several times, I mentioned that if we keep going around in circles, we will run out of gas, and suggested we postpone further embracing until we could make use of the couch in the company office at Buchanan Field. Great idea, but the romance abruptly ended when we discovered her husband waiting at the airport. I made note that he was much bigger than me and very well built. So when she tried to contact me a few days later, I did not return her calls and never saw her again. WHEW!

Dangerous events could occur on the ground, as well as in the air, when chartering. The story involves a regular customer that loved to charter Las Vegas trips to gamble, and I assume indulge in other Vegas activities. "Remember what happens in Vegas stays in Vegas." On one particular trip to Vegas, he told me not to stay over and fly home. About three days later, around midnight, he called saying he was ready to be picked up and flown home. However, he informed me he was now at Lindberg Field in San Diego. I arrived about two a.m. No one was in the airport waiting room but my customer, sound asleep in a chair.

Several attempts to awaken him failed, so I gently started shaking him by his coat lapels, when rolls of 100 dollar bills started falling from his jacket pockets. Thinking he was witnessing a mugging, a night security guard approached with handgun drawn. My customer awoke, just at that critical moment, and with a drunken slur hollered, "HI THERE, AL. LET'S GO HOME." The man had won the Trifecta at the Tijuana Racetrack and had thousands of dollars stuffed in all his pockets.

As dawn was breaking, we landed at his home airport. Since my big winner was still a bit under the weather, I locked him up in his car and headed home. How he got from Las Vegas to Tijuana is a mystery never solved, but I did get a generous tip, with some of those brand new crisp 100 dollar bills.

Such was the life of a young charter pilot circa the fifties.

Chapter Four
Eastern Airlines and Celebrities

In 1959, I was hired by Eastern Airlines and qualified as copilot on their Martin 404s and Convair 440s. These two planes were similar 44-passenger short haul airliners of the time, powered by two Pratt & Whitney 2,000 horsepower radial piston engines with a crew of three, pilot, copilot, and stewardess.

#10 MARTIN 404 AIRLINER

Eddie Rickenbacker, the famous WWI ace, was still chairman of the board. Captain Eddie's decree was: "Pilots are paid to fly, not play with autopilots." Therefore, no Eastern Airlines plane was equipped with an autopilot and every trip had to be hand flown. This created a very tedious workload for the flight crew, especially in heavy weather (a term used by pilots for bad or extreme flying conditions). I, in fact, became a human autopilot on a flight from Miami to New York City, aboard a Lockheed Constellation aircraft, the newest four-engine queen and pride of the Eastern Airlines fleet. The cockpit was configured with a small "jump seat" located directly behind the captain's chair. I was not a crew member and occupied the jump seat on a company pass. Shortly after reaching our assigned cruising altitude, the captain turned in his seat and asked, "Son, would you like to fly the ship for a while?" What an opportunity! He didn't have to ask twice! I switched places with him, and as I flew the airplane, he relaxed, had coffee and snacks, chatted with the stewardess, and made occasional trips through the passenger cabin.

Over the distance of the route, what appeared to be a great opportunity and a lot of fun turned out to be a lot of work! The captain would check the instruments occasionally and remind me to maintain our assigned altitude and heading, but other than that, the autopilot was engaged—me.

After graduation from copilot training in Miami, Florida, I was domiciled in New York City, where all junior copilots were sent. With my low seniority number, I only qualified as a reserve copilot. A reserve copilot was on a 24-hour call to fill in when the regular scheduled pilot was not available.

I sat by the phone for over a month after settling down in New York City. Finally, one stormy winter evening, the call came from Eastern Airlines. The voice said, "Report to La Guardia airport. You're scheduled on flight XXX." This flight was the red-eye special from New York City to Savannah, Georgia, with frequent stops along the way. I arrived at the

Eastern Air Lines terminal weather briefing room just as snowflakes began to fall.

A grouchy-looking pilot entered the room, and a weather briefer informed me that this was going to be my captain. I introduced myself as his copilot for the pending flight. He asked, "Ackerman, how long have you been flying the line?" My response was, "Captain, this is my very first trip." In obvious anguish, he threw up his arms and his shout echoed throughout the building: "Son of a bitch, the worst flying weather this winter, and they give me a damn green copilot." What little confidence I had remaining in performing my duties quickly flew out the window.

My first assignment was to go out on the ramp and preflight the aircraft. I couldn't afford a uniform overcoat and nearly froze to death with temperatures hovering near freezing. It was beginning to snow very hard, and we were being further delayed waiting to be de-iced.

As I gazed around the cockpit, I soon realized how much I had forgotten about the plane since my training in Miami several months prior. The long period since being checked out on both the Martin 404 and the Convair 440 caused the two airplanes systems to meld together and confusion ruled the day.

The flight continued to go downhill. Taxiing out for takeoff, my next job was to copy and correctly read back the Air Traffic Control (ATC) instrument flight plan clearance. I never retained a word after the initial radio transmission. All I recalled was: "ATC clears Eastern 630 to Philadelphia via . . ." Everything that came after that was lost, and there was a lot of other instructions that vapor locked in my mind as we rolled into position for takeoff. The captain grasped his mic and glared at me as he read back the clearance without taking a breath. The bastard had probably listened to that same airway routing instruction with the proper related waypoints hundreds of times. Copilot Ackerman was ready to join the stewardess in the cabin.

My next job was to trim the cowl flaps on the takeoff roll. Cowl flaps are doors on the engine compartment that open and close to regulate how much air flows around the engine for cooling. When they are fully open, they add considerable drag to the plane. Bringing the cowl flaps to a half-closed position, or trimmed, decreases drag on takeoff. I had also overlooked this important duty and fell further out of my captain's good graces. There was another unfriendly glare and a curt reminder from "Capitan Grouch" of another missed copilot assignment. My confidence continued to wane. What procedure would I mess up next?

We climbed through solid clouds and arrived at our cruising altitude en route to our first stop in Philadelphia. The plane started to pick up ice, and the captain called for windshield heat. At this point of the story, I must explain the de-icing system of a Martin 404 Airliner. The 404 was equipped with Janitrol (brand name) gas-fired heaters, which were supplied by the aircraft fuel system. These efficient heaters provided hot air for wing, tail, and cockpit de-icing. The cockpit windshield and side windows were double paned so hot air could be distributed efficiently. Only the copilot had access to the three controls to direct hot air in the cockpit. One was windshield heat, another for side window heat, and the third was floor heat.

The Lord was not with me that night. The instrument light to illuminate these controls was burned out, and I could not recall which control was which. I considered using my flight bag flash light, but was in fear of further annoying the captain and having to endure yet another lashing of his wrath. So, I randomly chose one of the three available levers and actuated it. After a short time, the captain reached up to touch the windshield and it was ICE COLD! I had actuated the side window heat by mistake. Perhaps not a simple mistake, as I had not a clue which lever controlled which area. He then shouted, "Damn it, Ackerman, the WINDSHIELD HEAT!" I selected another control, but, unfortunately, it turned out to be the control for the cabin floor heat, which, most likely, had not been used in years. Almost immediately, dust and debris of unknown origins began spewing all over the cockpit.

I was not sure at this juncture if there was a copilot ejection seat, but I was certainly hoping there was not. I was now addressed as "One Stupid Bastard," and he commanded at the top of his lungs, "WINDSHIELD HEAT." The last of my three attempts was thankfully the correct one, only in that it was the last control lever available.

The cockpit door was left open in those pre-911 days. The stewardess' station was in the rear of the passenger cabin. A short time later, I felt a hand on my shoulder. It was the stewardess, and she whispered in my ear, "Is everything all right?" The captain's ranting and raving apparently could be heard throughout the airplane. I wonder if those poor red-eyed passengers ever flew on Eastern Airlines again. So went the first leg of my first flight with the "Great Silver Fleet" known as Eastern Airlines.

After a sleepless layover in Savannah, Georgia, deep in the beauty of the Atlantic coast's low country, I lay there dreading that day's trip with Captain Grouch. The morning broke crisp and clear, and everything was lining up for a beautiful winter day on the East Coast. No need for my nemesis windshield heat to attack me that day. We were scheduled to return in a hopscotch pattern back up the coast through New York and all the way to upstate Massena, which was located on the Saint Lawrence River, and then on to our final destination at La Guardia Airport.

I had to tolerate my new cockpit buddy for the remainder of the trip, and although things went a little smoother, he never stopped chewing out my ass for one reason or another. At the end of the trip, I gave serious thoughts of quitting. Fortunately, subsequent trips were with captains who understood my apprenticeship, perhaps were able to recall their own rookie seasons, and so provided what was missing from my inaugural voyage.

These gentlemen aviators were not only good teachers, but they were excellent motivators, as they restored my self-confidence along with their positive comments regarding my natural flying skills. I existed on the very meager pay of 400 dollars a month at this point in my life. This did not go very far in New York City, even in 1959.

My seniority number was second from the bottom. Every time the airline cut back due to slow times in the industry, I was one of the first to be furloughed, not fired, but laid off without pay until recalled. After enduring several lengthy furloughs, I was flat broke and tendered my resignation to Eastern Airlines. Another disappointment, as I had planned to be the best captain on that Eastern Airlines ever had. As it turned out, in retrospect, leaving Eastern at that time turned out to be a blessing in disguise. Had I managed to stay with Eastern Airlines, I would have risen to the position of senior captain just four years from retirement as they filed for bankruptcy protection on March 9, 1989. During one of my furloughs, an opportunity arose to be Frank Sinatra's substitute copilot for his regular pilot on sick leave, to help crew his private Executive Martin 404. It was a surplus airliner converted into a flying night club. The aircraft interior was quite elaborate. There was a mid-cabin piano bar with twinkling star lights overhead and a very adequately stocked liquor cabinet. Included in this plush, custom interior was a convenient aft master bedroom. Mr. Sinatra always arrived with a bevy of Hollywood and Las Vegas VIPs, including stunning Hollywood starlets. Old Blue Eyes never knew I existed, and from what I observed, was not the friendliest of men to the hired help. That said, I certainly enjoyed the view from the cheap seats.

My first charter with a Hollywood movie star turned out to be Betty Hutton. She was an actress and comedienne, and extremely popular in the forties and fifties. She was known as the "Blonde Bombshell" and was best known for her film role as Annie Oakley in *Annie Get Your Gun*. She was past her prime at that time, but still a very attractive woman, though missing that vivacious attitude that had made her the darling of the silver screen for almost two decades. There was very little conversation between us during the flight. She appeared somewhat depressed. Later documentaries on her life and career mentioned that she did suffer from alcoholism and depression, and there was even an attempted suicide.

Another charter flight was a week-long tour with Steppenwolf, a Canadian-American musical rock group that was very popular in the sixties. Fighting off the groupies was a full-time endeavor. However, this trip turned out to be a bummer. After the second night's gig, the airplane broke down with no quick repair available. Much to my dismay, a not-too-well-liked competitor took over the remainder of the tour. Oh well, I was not into their music anyway.

In the years 1969 and 1970, I flew Conway Twitty and Hank Williams Jr., two legends of country and western music, on a tour with hopes of selling them an airplane. I was showing off the Howard Super Ventura, an aircraft converted from a Lockheed PV-1 Ventura Navy WWII bomber to an executive aircraft by The Dee Howard Company in the 1950s. She was piston powered by two Pratt and Whitney R-2800 radial engines, each producing 2,000 horsepower, with a cruising speed of 300 miles per hour. The Ventura had a large passenger cabin with stand-up headroom, plush seats looking out of large picture windows, and a full-service bar and lavatory. The former bomb bays had been converted to baggage storage, which would accommodate all the equipment their stage show needed to travel with.

#11 HOWARD SUPER VENTURA

My first tour was with Conway Twitty and the Twitty Birds. Big Joe was on the base guitar and Pork Chop on the drums and others made every gig an adventure, especially places like, Mankato, Minnesota, Cairo and Cicero, Illinois, where I always felt backing out of the auditorium was the better part of valor.

Big Joe would brag to the ladies that the plane they came in, piloted by yours truly, was so powerful that if it made a high speed pass down the runway, it would suck the pavement right out of the ground. He would then glance in my direction looking for my nod of approval. When one of the ladies asked for a demonstration, Big Joe quickly changed the subject to: "What are you doing after the show?" All performance payments were made in cash and carried only by Conway in a small leather satchel. I sincerely doubt the Internal Revenue agents in Washington were ever aware of this practice.

I was invited to dinner at Conway's home in Oklahoma City with his second wife, Temple Maxine, and a young son named Jimmy. The child was very athletic, following in his father's footsteps, who was a high school baseball star and had offers to try out with the Philadelphia Phillies; but, unfortunately before he could report, he was drafted by the army. We played football in the front yard, and the boy made some spectacular catches while running in full stride. In my humble opinion, he had the makings of a great wide receiver.

Conway had just opened his first Twitty Burger restaurant in Oklahoma City. I was obliged to sample several Twitty Burgers. A hamburger patty topped with cheese, two slices of bacon, and a deep fried, graham cracker crusted pineapple ring. With an airplane sale being number one on my agenda, I naturally gave Conway a glowing report on how delicious his burgers were. The burger eating public never shared my enthusiasm, and Twitty Burger went bankrupt in 1971, only two years after opening. Any chance of an airplane sale was lost with the failure of Twitty Burger.

I also toured with Hank Williams Jr., who was known as "Bocehphus" by country music fans everywhere. During the first performance of the tour, I was asked to sit on the front row of the auditorium, where they illuminated me in a spotlight and announced, "We are honored tonight to have in our presence Mr. Al Ackerman, vice president of Decca Records. If any young ladies in the audience would like an interview, Mr. Ackerman will be available backstage after the show." I never suspected there were so many untalented, but willing, young ladies in an audience. Hank and the crew seemed to enjoy a little fun at my expense, and for a short period of time, life was good as a "record label executive."

I spent several days in Nashville negotiating an aircraft sale with Hank's business manager. He was a huge man with a deep, raspy voice and had the appearance of a retired professional wrestler. He was against any aircraft purchase and, as a result, took a strong dislike towards me. I overheard several conversations between him and Hank Jr., within which he referred to me as, "Al Capone, the gangster." After some "touch and go negotiations," I did prevail and sold the Howard Super Ventura to Hank Jr. The band used the plane successfully on tour for several years.

These trips dedicated to selling the Howard Super Ventura were both demanding and sometimes chaotic. Some well-earned relief came when my copilot and I were deadheading between demonstrations with no passengers on board and came across a DC-3.

The venerable Douglas DC-3 was still in wide use as a corporate plane at this time. Remmert-Werner, a company in Saint Louis, Missouri, specialized in modifying surplus C-47s, which was the military version of the DC-3, to an executive aircraft. The modifications included a plush interior with large picture windows in the passenger cabin. We often encountered one of these executive DC-3s lumbering across the countryside at 165 miles per hour.

The Super Ventura was 125 miles per hour faster than the DC-3. I would maneuver the Ventura up along the side of the DC-3 and look for the boss relaxing in the catbird seat, hopefully gazing out his picture window, and when I had his undivided attention, I would shut down the engine and feather the propeller (zero thrust) that was within his view.

Our opposite engine was set at METO (Maximum Except Takeoff Power). In this configuration, we could not only keep up with the DC-3, we could fly a complete orbit around it. After completing the orbit, I would reposition the Ventura in view of the now wide-eyed boss, start up the shutdown engine, and give a salute of goodbye. I don't know if this ever enhanced the sales of the Super Ventura, but it had to make a definite impression. I'm sure the crew of the DC-3 had a few choice words for me, as I could observe some shaking fists pointed in our direction from their cockpit windows as we drew away.

This kind of flying bravado would be impossible to perform today. It would most likely result in the suspension or even revocation of my pilot license. At the time, it gave me genuine elation. If I could go back 36 years, I would do it all over again without giving it a second thought!

After that entire well-earned relief story, I have more celebrity episodes to tell. Paul Harvey, the famous radio commentator and host of the popular radio show *News and Comment* and its daily segment referred to as "And Now, the Rest of the Story" was another client of mine. During my first flight with America's most favorite storyteller since Will Rogers, I went back to the cabin to offer Mr. Harvey a beverage, only to find him sitting in his underwear. WHOA! Should I high tail it back to the cockpit? No, he had the practice of hanging his trousers over the back of another seat to prevent them from wrinkling between appointments. He was an affable and very friendly person, not consumed with his own celebrity. I had expected his reputation to follow him onboard, as a man of quick temper and outbursts. I never saw that side of him. To me, he was a consummate gentleman. Perhaps it had more to do with his personal safety and my growing reputation among the elite as the world's best pilot. Okay, that's a stretch, but it was always my ultimate goal.

I flew famous car racer, A.J. Foyt, four-time winner of the Indy 500 (1961, 1964, 1967, 1977), to several Indy 500 and Daytona 500 car races. At one time during this period, I was invited to visit the pits during races, staying well out of the way of the hectic pit stops. I found out A.J. was very superstitious about several things. Mr. Foyt considered use of the color green on a racecar to bring bad luck, and he became very uneasy if any green cars were in the lineup. When Jim Clark, The Flying Scotsman, showed up at the 1963 Indy 500 race with his rear engine English racecar painted in British racing green, A.J. was one unhappy camper. He had another superstition regarding the wishing of good luck prior to a race, and a "thumbs up" jester was barely tolerated.

After practice runs at Daytona one year, A.J. invited me and several others to ride around the track in his 1978 Lincoln Town Car. After two laps at full speed, the Lincoln was spent, and by the time we pulled into the pits, the tires were actually smoking and close to failure. A.J. got out of the car and looked at the tires and said, "You guys see what crap the tire companies put on your cars?" He then hollered over to the pit crew chief, "Hey Jack, put another set of tires on the Lincoln."

In 1973, I flew a San Antonio car owner and his fans to the NASCAR race in Talladega, Alabama, in a model 1121 Jet Commander. Instrument approaches were in progress at Talladega due to low clouds and poor visibilities.

#12 AUTHOR WITH JET COMMANDER 1121 CIRCA 1970

There was no control tower at the airport, so closing your flight plan had to be done by telephone on completion of a safe landing. I closed my plan, as required, and was arranging ground transportation when a very irate pilot stormed into the terminal demanding to see that SOB jet commander captain.

I presented myself, and he started cursing and accusing me of not closing my flight plan, forcing him into a holding pattern for over 30 minutes before being cleared for his approach. I replied, "I closed my G D flight plan. Get the hell out of my face, and who in the 'frap' are you?" (You, the reader, can define the real F-word used in this heated exchange.) I then clenched my fist, ready to deliver a punch if necessary. He replied, "My name is Bobby Allison, and I'm late at the track." I was taken aback for a moment, unclenched my fist, held out my hand in friendship, and said, "Welcome to Talladega, Mr. Allison, have a safe race and hope to see you in the winner's circle!"

Minnie Pearl, of Grand Ole Opry fame, franchised Minnie Pearl Fried Chicken, a fast food restaurant chain during the 1970s. Her company operated a Howard 250, a high-performance version of an original 1940s vintage Lockheed Lodestar modified by the Dee Howard Company. The plane was scheduled for maintenance at the Howard facilities in San Antonio, Texas, where I was employed at the time. Minnie's copilot was unavailable, so I was dispatched to Nashville to fly the Howard 250 back with Minnie's captain. The flight proceeded routinely. The captain seemed knowledgeable and proficient; however, it was dark by the time we approached San Antonio.

Low ceilings and restricted visibilities mandated an instrument approach. During the approach, the captain kept calling for brighter instrument lights until I told him that was all we had. He then pulled out a book of matches and held a burning match close to the instruments. When the match started burning his fingers, it was dropped to the cockpit floor, creating a nice fire hazard. Then he then struck another match that also ended up on the cockpit floor. The instrument approach was very poorly flown, and at one point I was tempted to take over the controls. This would have been a big no-no, possibly damaging my company's relations with Minnie Pearl. I made a mental note to never fly with that gentleman again after dark.

Bill Lear, one of the greatest entrepreneurs of our time, helped design the first practical car radio that came to be known as Motorola. He designed many innovative and breakthrough technologies in aircraft radios, autopilots, and even the eight-track tape deck. His most well-known project was the development and certification of the Learjet in the 1960s.

My boss at the time, Dee Howard, and I were deeply involved with Learjets. Dee had a long association with Bill Lear and they were good competitive friends. I demonstrated

#13 DEE HOWARD, AUTHOR, BILL LEAR CIRCA 1975

several of the FAA-certified performance improvement modifications that Howard had developed for the Learjet to Mr. Lear. I do not believe Mr. Lear really enjoyed someone fooling around with his pet project. He never had much to say after the demos, but I observed from his demeanor in the cockpit during my demo that he was impressed.

Mr. Howard and I were often invited to the Lear facilities in Reno, Nevada, for a business lunch. Bill's idea of lunch was hamburgers and grilled onions, personally cooked on a commercial-sized grill located in the corner of his office. On one visit, Bill was in the preliminary design of a new corporate jet he named "the Allegro." Several different manufacturers were interested in the design. Within an hour of our lunch, three different parties called. Bill's sales pitch was a little different to fit each occasion. I sat there taking a lesson in an excellent display of salesmanship. The Allegro design was eventually sold to a Canadian Company and serves corporate aviation today as the "Challenger Series" of business jets.

Years later, I was honored to be selected to participate in a three Learjet formation flyover at Bill Lear's funeral in Reno. The funeral home was located in the middle of the town. FAA regulations limited all flights to a minimum altitude of 1,000 feet over a populated area. I flew right wingman in the formation and was glued onto my leader so that I could maintain a tight position. I then noticed that my copilot was getting uncomfortable. I took a quick glance toward the ground to discover the formation was roaring across downtown Reno at an altitude of no more than two hundred feet. I expected the FAA to be waiting for us at the airport, but we never heard a word regarding our altitude violation. Perhaps Mr. Lear was watching over us.

Our flyover consisted of two passes over the funeral home. The second pass was made on a westerly heading in keeping with the tradition of a dearly departed aviator. Pilots refer to the passing of a fellow aviation member simply as "He has gone west."

One of my friends who attended the funeral was walking back to his car, which was parked several blocks away, when he came across a family in their front yard sitting in lawn chairs looking to the sky. They asked him, "Do you know when that air show is coming back?"

Moya Lear, Bill Lear's widow, sent me a photo of the flyby with the following inscription:

Dear Al: None of us will ever forget this moment. He left his wonderful Spirit and you helped so much in saying Aloha.

Thank You,

Moya Lear

Dated May 17, 1978

This item remains chief among my 62 years of memorabilia that adorn my study in the high mountains of New Mexico.

Chapter Five
Politicians and a Former President

Edmund Muskie, senator from Maine, was the Democratic nominee for president in 1972. During his campaign, I flew him up and down the East Coast from Maine to Florida for political rallies. We would normally arrive back in Portland, Maine, for the night. During my short time with his campaign, I had more than my fill of Maine lobster.

Senator Muskie was a perfect gentleman and was very understanding of a few missed appointments due to some aircraft mechanical problems. The senator's political opponents uncovered some damaging information about his wife having been treated for mental issues. The senator chose not to engage in the political mudslinging and dropped out of the race. This was unfortunate for, in my humble opinion, he would have made a great president. Pardon the political interruption, but Edmund Muskie was a statesman and put his family well ahead of his political ambitions. It seems that we have a different set of values in Washington today.

Dolph Briscoe, governor of Texas from 1973 to 1979, and his wife, Janey "B," owned a Howard 500 aircraft with "Janey B" painted in bold letters across the nose. The aircraft was one of only 17 Howard 500s ever built. To the best of my knowledge, he was the only state governor to ever operate that aircraft. After he left the Governor's Mansion, I made quite a few trips with the governor and his wife to his ranch in Uvalde, Texas. They were always the perfect host and hostess during these trips.

I had the opportunity to fly former Vice President and then Senator Hubert H. Humphrey on a week of trips through the Midwest. During this trip, we encountered the worst flying weather imaginable. Almost daily we were dodging thunderstorms, landing with minimum ceilings and visibilities, or managing other difficult situations. We arrived exhausted after each flight. Not one scheduled appointment was missed. Yet there was not one word of appreciation offered from Mr. Humphrey or any of his associates. It could not have been more different than my time with Senator Muskie.

Speaker of the House Jim Wright and some other dignitaries that were less notable with names long forgotten were of about the same demeanor. The typical politician and the staffs that surrounded them were totally consumed with themselves and not very agreeable traveling companions.

In 1969, after his presidency and subsequent retirement to the Johnson Ranch in Johnson City, Texas, President Lyndon Baines Johnson, through a business acquisition, inherited a Howard Super Ventura aircraft. The plane was identical to the one purchased by Hank Williams Jr., as described in Chapter Four. This old WWII flying machine had been expertly converted for civilian use by the Dee Howard Company in the 1950s.

One fall afternoon, while I was sitting in Dee Howard's personal office at the San Antonio International Airport, the phone rang. Mr. Howard, at one point in the conversation, put his hand over the phone and remarked, "Somebody is pulling my leg representing himself as the president of the

United States!" The conversation continued, and Mr. Howard was finally convinced that he was indeed speaking to the real LBJ. He looked at me with a surprised expression and said, "That was President Johnson on the phone, and it looks like we are going to crew, maintain, and base his new Howard Super Ventura here at our facilities in San Antonio.

Little did we know then that the privilege of managing the Super Ventura for the former president would became a substantial burden and "contribution." LBJ did maintain fueling facilities for the aircraft at his ranch in Johnson City, Texas; however, everything else we took care of gratis (free of charge).

The Ventura had a large passenger cabin with stand-up head room, plush seats looking out of large picture windows, and a full service bar and lavatory. LBJ favored all these features, and since it was faster than other private aircraft that were available to him, it became his first choice for family outings and personal trips.

Since no one in the LBJ entourage knew how to fly a Super Ventura, the privilege of escorting President Johnson fell to me. And so the saga of flying LBJ and family in a WWII bomber came to be. Since the plane was not based at the Johnson ranch but in San Antonio, it had to be flown to the LBJ ranch three days prior to any LBJ trip to be secured by the Secret Service and to have world-wide communications installed. After each flight, I would then be driven back and forth from the ranch to my office or home as needed by the Secret Service.

The Secret Service called me the evening before my first trip and requested that I be ready to be picked up at 6:00 a.m. the following morning. I replied that I was aware of the schedule and offered directions to my house. Their curt response: "Mr. Ackerman, we know exactly where you live." I was tempted to check around the house and in my attic for listening devices, and took a glance outside to see if any black colored SUVs with tinted windows were parked across the street.

Every trip was conducted on a Code I flight plan, meaning all air traffic give way, important VIP on board. I can only imagine the expression on other pilot's faces if they only knew that the Code I aircraft was a WWII bomber. We always landed at military bases with much military fanfare. Many of the trips were to College Bowl games when Texas teams were playing and the Super Bowl, especially when the Dallas Cowboys were involved. When attending these events, my ID tag was the same as that of the Secret Service, and I could have sat on the Cowboy bench without being challenged. However, I always sat with LBJ's group, but tried to sit far from LBJ, just in case someone in the stadium had an "old bone" to pick with the former president.

One memorable Super Bowl trip was the 1972 game between the Dallas Cowboys and the Miami Dolphins, held at Tulane Stadium in New Orleans. As always, we landed at a military facility, on this occasion the New Orleans Naval Air Station. We were directed to park next to an air force Lockheed Jet Star, an aircraft in use at that time for top military brass and transport of VIPs. I accompanied the presidential party and Secret Service to the game and to the delight of LBJ, the Cowboys won 24–3. On return to the naval air station, I immediately went to the Super Ventura to check the passenger cabin condition for our return to the Johnson Ranch. I noticed LBJ and Lady Bird being escorted to the air force Jet Star. I was then informed by the Secret Service they would be going on to Washington, DC, and not returning with the rest of the family.

I went back to my clean up chores when the cabin door flew open and in barged LBJ with a clothes bag over his shoulder. He had worn his usual western attire to the game, including his favorite Stetson hat and cowboy boots. The clothes bag contained a dark blue business suit and accessories he was planning to wear for his trip to DC. He caught me by surprise and said, "Ackerman, I can't change clothes in that G D small Jet Star." "Ackerman" was the only way LBJ ever addressed me. He then proceeded to get undressed. I made a suggestion that he might like me to close the cabin window curtains to afford some privacy. I did, and the Secret Service personnel watching from outside the plane went into a panic mode, running around the plane, trying to look in, and shouting instructions. One knocked on the cabin door and LBJ, in a few choice words, told him to wait outside. LBJ, half undressed, decided to make use of the aircraft lavatory. Without any air circulation in the plane, the cabin atmosphere became a bit odorous.

LBJ was really not well at the time and needed my help in changing outfits. I was now undergoing on-the-job training as a presidential valet. I had to help take off his boots and then tie his shoes. He was unable to knot his tie correctly, so I was instructed to reach around his shoulders from behind and perform this duty while he observed in the lavatory mirror that it was done to his satisfaction. LBJ stood tall in front of me after finishing the change of clothing and asked, "Ackerman, how do I look?" I responded, "Mr. President, you look great."

His last request before leaving the plane was that I take special care of his Stetson hat and place it onboard where it wouldn't be crushed. I assured the president it would be taken care of. This had to be one of the more critical assignments of my life. I opened the cabin door where several Secret Service men greeted me with unfriendly glares and wished my impeccably dressed president (with a flawless necktie) a safe journey.

On many trips the LBJ family brought aboard picnic baskets full of fried chicken, potato salad, and all the trimmings. I'm sure there was plenty to go around, but no one in the family ever once offered a bite to the crew. Perhaps they feared we could not steer the plane and eat fried chicken at the same time.

The cockpit had a third crew seat, called the observer chair. When Luci Baines and her first husband, Pat Nugent, were on board, Mr. Nugent always spent the entire flight in the observer chair. He really appeared not that interested in the cockpit proceedings. I always suspected that he needed a lot of space from LBJ residing in the main cabin. By the way, as long as he stayed in the cockpit, he didn't get any fried chicken either.

During these trips, somewhere en route, LBJ would holler up to the cockpit, "Ackerman, come back here." I turned over the controls to my copilot and returned to the passenger cabin. LBJ gave me a firm look and said, "I have something to give you." He presented me with a lovely gold presidential seal tie pin, assuring me there were only a few left and I should have one. This same scenario was repeated on numerous trips over the years. I always accepted the gift graciously, never wanting to embarrass the president by reminding him I had a sizeable presidential pin collection developing. My family and a few friends are all in possession of gold presidential seal tie pins. LBJ was certainly the consequential politician of his time.

One of the Secret Service agents I became most familiar with told me one day, in the strictest confidence, that if you mess up in the Secret Service, you wind up at the Johnson Ranch. I always suspected that other duties besides guarding the president were required. The scuttlebutt was that he expected agents to perform standard ranch hand chores, such as mending fences, herding cows, and perhaps, last but not least, hauling manure. In truth, it was more than scuttlebutt, as I personally observed some of these chores being accomplished.

One gloomy Texas winter day, I was summoned to the ranch for lunch. Several days before, in fog and poor visibility, a family operated helicopter en route from Austin Texas to the Johnson ranch flew into some high voltage transmission lines, causing it to crash, killing the pilot. LBJ had ordered the flight, even though the pilot had stated his concerns regarding the flying weather. LBJ felt guilty that his decision to override the pilot's objections to the flight had led to the accident. Somewhere along the way, in the eyes of LBJ, I had become his aviation consultant. During that lunch, we had a long discussion about the tragedy, and I hoped my comments somewhat relieved his guilty feelings. That was the last time I saw LBJ. He was quite ill at the time and passed away several weeks later.

Our services no longer needed with his passing, that old reliable bomber and I parted company. She most likely went to a salvage yard, and I was left with my memories of the years with LBJ. Those memories returned in a flash on a recent fly-in gathering in Fredericksburg, Texas. My wife, Debbie, and I, along with a group of other attendees, decided to take a tour of the Johnson Ranch, which is now a National Historic Park.

Talk about déjà vu! None of the furnishings or decor in the ranch house had been changed since my last time there. The dining room chair I sat in during meals was in exactly the same place and position. The leather easy chair and ottoman in the den where LBJ sat during that last visit was unchanged. The ranch vehicles used to transport me back and forth to the ranch were displayed in a garage museum. A Lockheed Jet Star on static display was maintained in pristine condition. Walking around the Jet Star, I had a thought: Wouldn't it be great if that old Super Ventura could be on display next door? After all, it had a place in LBJ's history, as well. The airstrip that the old bomber and I landed on numerous times had not changed in the least. I came away from my visit to the Johnson Ranch with a strong, yet unexplained, sense of foreboding, and I was glad when the tour ended.

My adventures with LBJ took place during a prime time of my life. The thoughts of illness or even death were the furthest things from my mind. It was now thirty-eight years later. I vividly recalled that last visit with an ailing president, sitting in that same leather easy chair, just weeks before he passed away. It caused a feeling of vulnerability to my own aging and chances of deteriorating health and overall wellbeing. Those memories best explain my uncomfortable mood during the tour. The rest of the fly-in activities were enjoyable, but I made a mental note that one visit to the Johnson Ranch National Historic Park would suffice for the remainder of my life.

Chapter Six
Survival in the Deep

In November 1966, while en route to the Caribbean to pick up an executive client, my life changed forever. Similar to most flights, things were routine, with not a lot to do, until there was! The old saying among aviators that flying is "hours and hours of sheer boredom punctuated by a moment of stark terror" came to bear in a horrific way for me that day.

My moment came on that dark and moonless night on an overwater approach of less than ten miles to my destination airport. Without warning or time to react, my jet flew through a flock of migrating seabirds. Multiple strikes caused the aircraft to lose roll control. I desperately tried to keep the aircraft in the air, but was unsuccessful, resulting in a descending 360-degree spiral into the sea at over 300 miles per hour. The aircraft virtually disintegrated upon impact, and by some miraculous act of God, I was expelled through the destruction and flying debris, and yet still strapped in my pilot's seat.

The chance of survival in an airplane plunging into the sea at 300 miles per hour was probably one in a million. Hitting the water at that speed would be like driving an automobile straight into a brick wall at 100 miles per hour. The ejection path had to follow some kind of a decelerating arc or I could have never survived my impact with the water.

I regained consciousness while still strapped in the seat, covered with jet fuel, and surrounded by small pieces of the airplane. The impact was so severe my shoes, socks, all my jewelry, and shirt were gone; only my trousers and a Saint Christopher medal worn on a chain around my neck remained. I detached myself from the seat as it started to sink and felt around my body to check for missing parts. I was all there except I had no feeling or use of my left arm, so I became a one-armed swimmer. In a short time, several Coast Guard Albatross amphibian aircraft appeared overhead, dropping flares. Small boats with searchlights appeared in the distance. Unfortunately, nobody came close to finding me in that large body of water. I was then alone in the dark, with only God and complete silence.

At one point I arose to the top of a wave and could see the lights of the shoreline in the far distance. I made the decision that, in order to survive, I had to set a distance record for one-arm swimming. In reality, that feat was impossible. That far shore was at least five long miles away.

I managed to grasp some floating pieces of shattered wood that were the remains of the aircraft's interior cabinets and wrapped my legs around them to help me keep afloat. The hours passed, the jagged edges of the cabinet pieces kept lacerating my legs, and I could no longer hold on to them. Unknown things occasionally bumped my legs, terrorizing me. More time passed, and I grew weaker and extremely thirsty. Occasionally a rain shower would pass overhead, and I would hold my mouth open to the sky, trying to catch raindrops. I can only imagine what a pitiful sight I must have been. Those distant lights didn't seem to be getting any closer, and at times I gave up and beseeched the Almighty to forgive my transgressions.

I said my goodbyes and slipped beneath the waves. A

little voice kept telling me "do not drown out here alone; no one will know what happened," so I kept trying. More hours passed, and finally on one of my rides to the top of a wave, a new groups of lights appeared. I determined that the new lights were, in fact, a large ship that was going to pass between me and the shore. With my remaining strength, I swam toward the ship hollering for help. It was now the early hours of morning before sunrise. Most fortunate for me, sailors were on deck, probably having a smoke break, and heard my cries.

In that emptiness, sound carried so far. To my joy, I could hear their footsteps running up a metal gangway, while shouting in Spanish, "Capitan! Capitan!"

The ship became completely illuminated with horns blaring. However, by the time the ship came to a stop, it was much farther away than I could ever hope to swim. Intervention from a "higher source" came to my rescue again as someone aboard that South American cargo ship had the brilliant idea to call ashore for smaller boats to come and start circling the ship in larger and larger orbits. It seemed an eternity was passing as the boats, with each growing circle, came closer. "Oh God, don't let them miss me. I have nothing left to give."

A light suddenly appeared, shining and searching the waves close to me. With my last remaining breath I shouted, "I'm over here! I'm over here!" A voice came out of the darkness. "There he is! Watch out; don't run over him!" A strong hand firmly grasped mine, lifted me into the boat, and I was delivered from that watery grave. No words in any language spoken on this planet can describe the feeling I felt when that hand touched mine.

My injuries included a compound fracture of the left arm humerus bone, resulting in considerable radial nerve damage, and a broken left collarbone. I had fractured ribs on my left side, one that penetrated and collapsed my left lung. I had numerous deep lacerations on my legs and torso. The superbly talented attending doctors, nurses, and therapists that put me back together were amazed that somehow I had escaped serious internal, head, and spinal injuries from the tremendous impact of the crash. I have always believed this blessing had to come from God. He had more for me to accomplish.

A long recuperation period lay ahead of me. Depression overwhelmed me. I had only limited use of my left arm. I could not lift my left wrist or open my hand. Would they ever become fully functional again? Would I ever fly again? Piloting an airplane was all I knew how to do!

During this difficult time, someone suggested I should attend a weekend Catholic retreat where I could meditate and give thanks to God for my miraculous survival. I decided to go and arranged a private meeting with the attending priest. Often fighting back emotional tears, I related my story and asked, "Father please pray for me." His response was, "My son, as close as you have been to God, please say a prayer for me." That statement touched the very depths of my soul. It gave me the will to work hard at rehabilitating my crippled arm and hand and rebuild my shattered life as best I could.

My rehabilitation program was arduous at best. I could not lift my left arm any higher than my shoulder or raise my wrist or open my left hand at my first physical therapy session. Progress was measured in very small degrees over the ensuing year. The nerve damage to my arm and hand were extensive; any movement at all was very difficult.

I had issues with swelling due to the pooling of fluids in my left hand and was forced to wear a brace on my forearm to keep the wrist and hand elevated. An inflatable balloon type glove was worn at night to ease the swelling.

Two times per week I presented myself to "Helga," my physical therapist. She was relentless in her demands on me. Her name was not really Helga, but it seemed fitting for such a rough and domineering therapist. I was instructed to lay my left forearm sideways on a solid wooden plank lined with talcum powder, with my wrist curled inward. Then, I was "encouraged" to lift my wrist. The problem was I did not have the ability to accomplish her demands. She would continue to raise her voice, and intensify her demands, to the point I really wanted to lift that limp wrist with my good hand and slap her across the face.

As my frustrations and dislike for my therapist grew, week to week, my ability to raise my wrist remained unattainable. Some eight months later, without warning, during a therapy session when it was least expected, I managed a very slight movement of the wrist. Helga was overwhelmed by this small victory, and for a moment I thought she might hug and kiss me. My intense resentment of her turned immediately to gratitude. It took several more months of therapy before I regained full motion of my wrist and hand. After a year of intense physical therapy now behind me, I was now ready to move on to the next chapter of my life.

In the next year, I had to come to terms with a number of factors that developed from this accident. In addition to regaining my loss of mobility and the need to rise above a very depressive state of mind, I suffered many sleepless nights and constant thoughts about what I, as the pilot, could have done better to save the aircraft from its total destruction.

It was, perhaps, the most difficult year of my life, but I am confident this experience, as horrible as it was, allowed me to refocus my career and life. I learned, as a result of this experience, that whatever I faced from that point forward seemed insignificant in comparison to what I had overcome.

It is ironic that the Saint Christopher medal that survived that horrific crash was eventually destined to repose in the ocean. Several years after the accident while on a family holiday, the medal was lost surfing off the beach at Mazatlan, Mexico. Yet to this day, its replacement has never left my body.

Chapter Seven
The Dee Howard Years

Once my medical rehabilitation was complete, and I was able to pass my flight physical, I was hired by the Dee Howard Company of San Antonio, Texas, in 1968. The Dee Howard Company no longer manufactured the Howard line of aircraft. It was a maintenance, aircraft engineering, and design company. Initially, I was employed as a pilot, and as with many small companies, anything that needed doing was within my job description. During my first years with the company, I started the process of becoming qualified on the Learjet and Jet Commander aircraft, for which the company was developing new safety enhancements.

To qualify as pilot in command of a Learjet, one must pass a written and oral exam and take a check ride with an FAA-designated examiner. The check ride consisted mostly of emergency procedures. One of those procedures was an emergency descent simulating loss of cabin pressure at high attitude and getting the aircraft to a low, breathable altitude as quickly as possible. My instructor cautioned me that check rides were being failed because pilots were not descending fast enough in the emergency descent procedure. I had this on my mind when, at 41,000 feet altitude, the examiner called out "pressurization failure!"

The proper procedure was to immediately don your oxygen mask, close both power levers to idle, deploy the spoilers (small panels that open on top of the wings to destroy lift), extend the landing gear to increase drag, roll the airplane into a steep bank to reduce G-forces, and dive vertically for the ground. I had been practicing, and had precisely performed these tasks in seconds, and we were headed straight down.

The examiner was in shock and hollered at the top of his lungs, "That's enough! That's enough! Recover to level flight!" I passed my check ride with flying colors.

In the next few years as the company grew, I was promoted to the position of president of the sales division. I did a lot of travel and performed countless demonstrations of several important engineering safety enhancements to the Learjet and other corporate jets.

In 1974, The Dee Howard Company designed and certified thrust reversers for the model 20 series Learjet. Prior to that time, only drag chutes were optional equipment to assist in stopping on slick runways when braking action was poor to nil. Drag chutes were only effective if deployed immediately on touchdown. Many were deployed late and provided no effective stopping power. Therefore, some Learjets experienced runway overruns.

My responsibilities, as president of Dee Howard aircraft sales, included the demonstration and sale of the new thrust reversers. Further, Howard Learjet modifications (the Mark II system, XR system, and thrust reversers for the Model 30 Series Learjet) would be my responsibility to sell and demo in the following years.

The 20 series thrust reversers was a very successful program. My demonstrations of a V1 abort were the most rewarding. V1 is the calculated speed at takeoff where a decision must be made to abort the takeoff should one engine fail or continue on one engine to achieve V2 (safe lift off speed). At any speed below or at V1, one should abort the takeoff; at above V1, one should continue accelerating to V2 (safe lift-off single engine flying speed). A crucial, instantaneous decision must be made by the pilot. I would accelerate to exactly V1 speed and shut down one engine and deploy the thrust reverser on the remaining engine. The stopping effect was impressive, without directional control problems and with minimal braking necessary to bring the aircraft to a safe stop. This V1 demo sold almost every customer on purchasing our reversers. I probably hold the record for the most V1 aborts achieved in a series 20 Learjet.

A short time later, Dee Howard certified thrust reversers on the Model 1121 Jet Commander, which was another early generation private jet competitive to the Learjet. The 1121 earned the nickname "Lead Sled," being several thousand pounds heavier than a comparable Learjet. It was somewhat underpowered, requiring much longer runways for takeoff and landing. If any early model private jet needed thrust reversers, it was definitely the 1121 Jet Commander. The V1 abort demo in the Lead Sled brought tears of joy to Jet Commander pilots, and every demo resulted in a sale. I have no doubt I hold the record for the number of V1 aborts in the 1121 Jet Commander, as well.

I would put on my Learjet hat and head out for a week of demonstrations throughout the country and then return home for a couple of days of rest and recreation. The following Monday mornings, I would put on my Jet Commander hat and head out once again.

A ritual was developed on departing for another week of demonstrations. I would look over to my copilot and say, "Well, we're off again to screw up another demo." He responded with a mischievous grin, and then commented, "Or we'll demonstrate another screw up!"

The next unexpected Learjet improvement project for The Dee Howard Company turned out to be the Howard Raisbeck Mark II system. The 20 series Lear had very poor stall characteristics. Stalling, commonly misunderstood in an aircraft, has nothing to do with the engines stopping. An aircraft stall occurs when there is a decrease in airflow over the wing and then lift is lost, causing the stall.

Most airplanes have a natural aerodynamic buffeting that occurs when approaching a stall, giving the pilot ample time to lower the nose and stabilize the aircraft, avoiding a stall. A proper stall recovery enables a minimum loss of altitude, critical to the survival of the aircraft if the stall occurs close to the ground. The original design of the Learjet did not provide any aerodynamic buffeting and had to be certified with an electrically activated stick shaker and pusher.

Upon approaching a stall, the shaker would activate, thereby simulating natural buffeting. If recovery was not then achieved, the pusher would activate automatically, lowering the nose of the aircraft. Stall recoveries were always made at the shaker. No pilot would ever wait long enough for the pusher to activate because, prior to the pusher, the aircraft had a habit of violently rolling off to the right or to the left, and never the same way twice.

The Mark II system modification came from an outsider. Jim Raisbeck was a graduate of Purdue University's aeronautical engineering school and had worked for Boeing Aircraft in their high lift devices department. He was told by friends who were Learjet pilots about the aircraft's poor stall characteristics.

Jim was virtually unknown in aviation circles and eager to make his mark in aircraft design and modification. With his natural abilities, plus the knowledge he gained during his tenure with Boeing, Jim had an idea how to correct the Learjet stall problems. The design also provided a significant reduction in required takeoff and landing speeds. His answer was a new, thicker radius wing leading edge with stall turbulators and other aerodynamic improvements. After some successful preliminary test flights, he went to Learjet management at Wichita, Kansas, to sell his design. Raisbeck left empty handed. The Lear engineering department convinced management he was an outside upstart novice with no credibility.

Raisbeck was familiar with The Dee Howard Company and the successful Learjet reverser program. He presented his idea to Dee Howard. It turned out to be a perfect undertaking between the two parties. Dee Howard thrived on this type of aircraft performance improvement program and had the resources to pay for it. In less than six months, a short time by industry standards, the test program was completed, and the Howard Raisbeck Mark II system (MKII) was FAA certified. I was chosen to be the MK II demonstration pilot.

The MK II demo flights became some of the most enjoyable and fun flying in my entire career. Aircraft controllers and other pilots were both amazed and confused at how well a MKII-equipped Lear could fit in the landing pattern with slower aircraft and land in such short distances.

The first major airshow to see the MKII perform was held at Reading, Pennsylvania, in 1976. My routine was to execute a maximum climb after a short field takeoff, followed by a low level high-speed pass.

The real eye-opener was a figure eight maneuver at minimum landing speed with the landing gear and landing flaps extended, all executed while staying within the airport boundaries. A short field landing with a stop in front of the grandstand and backing up the Lear with the thrust reversers concluded my act. There were numerous Learjet pilots watching my demonstration, and several told me later that they had to turn away during the figure eight maneuver, convinced I would stall and crash at any moment.

#14 1976 READING PA. AIR SHOW

As much fun as I had showing off the slow flight capabilities of the MKII, my demonstration of stalls to veteran Learjet pilots was my ultimate delight. Most really didn't want to witness my demo but were too macho to refuse. I would perform full aerodynamic stalls with the shaker and pusher system turned off. The MKII system produced the natural buffeting so long missing in the standard airplane.

As we approached the stall, I would observe the knuckles of my potential buyer turn white, clutching the copilot seat armrest, anticipating a wild ride. To their amazement, the stall was straightforward and docile. After the stall recovery was completed, the white knuckles turned to wide grins, and more than one captain asked, "Al, can we do that again?" The "white knuckles to grins" scenario was repeated demonstration after demonstration. I probably hold the record for the number of full aerodynamic stalls preformed in a model 20 Learjet.

The Mark II was a great success and impressed the boys at Learjet so much they came to San Antonio for a meeting. They congratulated our team for a great achievement and stated they would fire their entire engineering department.

But, the real news was the decision to make the MKII standard equipment on all new production Learjets. However, this never happened. I am sure their finance department argued that too much money would go to an outside vendor, and the engineering department, pleading for survival, sold the idea that they could design a better modification in-house, and preserving the credibility of the company.

Rumors circulated throughout the industry that Learjet was to announce a new improvement modification they named the Century III system. The Century III system so closely duplicated the MKII that a lawsuit between the two companies ensued. A settlement was reached whereby Learjet had to pay Howard-Raisbeck a royalty on every Century III system installed on new production aircraft through a certain number of serial numbers. The Century III was also offered as a retrofit, but never competed successfully in that market against the MKII.

I test flew the Century III Lear, and without bias I found it didn't come close to matching the performance and docile handling characteristics of the MKII system. Stan Grayson, a friend employed by Howard as a test pilot during MKII certification, Jim Raisbeck, and I are, to the best of my knowledge, the only survivors to this piece of aviation history.

An unexpected plus for the MKII system was, with a slight power reduction after takeoff, it had the ability to meet Stage II noise restrictions standards. In those years, these noise restrictions were in effect at the larger airports in response to public noise complaints. Today more stringent noise restrictions are in effect. These requirements have generally been met with the advancements in airframe and engine design.

The ability for the MKII system to meet noise requirements was an unexpected bonus during a demonstration trip to the West Coast. We had been demonstrating in the Los Angeles area, and our next appointment was in San Jose, California. Running about thirty minutes late, I was concerned about missing our next client. On our final approach to San Jose, I noticed that our customer's hangar, identified by their company logo, was located just off the approach end of our landing runway.

The runway had a 1,200 feet overrun. I requested permission from the control tower to land on the overrun. This would save considerable minutes of taxi time. The tower controller most likely had never received this request by any jet airplane and was rendered speechless. There was no response from the controller, either positive or negative, and I was now committed to land. I performed my best short field landing technique, rolled up onto the runway threshold, and taxied the short distance to what I hoped would be my waiting customer.

I was briefing the captain on our forthcoming demo when cars with flashing lights pulled up in front of the hangar. The airport manager burst into the room, demanding what idiot just landed a Learjet on his runway overrun endangering everyone. I stood forward and received a verbal thrashing until I had a chance to explain the MKII-equipped Learjet's new capabilities, including meeting Stage II noise requirements. That got his immediate attention since the San Jose airport was located in a very noise-sensitive area. We agreed on departure to perform our noise reduction takeoff, and he would closely monitor all his noise monitoring equipment.

A few weeks later, I received a letter from the San Jose airport manager full of praise that we had met Stage II with flying colors. How thankful he was that we had made him aware of the MKII Learjet's improved performance. I was welcome to come back and land on his runway overrun anytime.

#15 HOWARD-RAISBECK MAGAZINE AD CIRCA 1970-80

Chapter Eight
Thrusters, the General, and the Amante

Upon completing the company tour throughout the USA, Canada, and Mexico, The Dee Howard demo crew embarked on a South American thrust reverser sales tour. To the best of our knowledge, there were no Jet Commander aircraft operating in South America at the time, so we focused on the 20 series Learjet, which was powered by two early technology GE CJ-610 turbo jet engines.

These engines were very reliable, but, as with all early jet engines, they consumed fuel at a very high rate. Our company demonstrator was a Model 23 Learjet serial number 98, registration number N5D, and it had a maximum range of three hours with a 30 minute reserve. This relatively short range meant many frequent fuel stops.

#16 LEARJET MODEL 23 REGISTRATION NO. N5D

Our flight plan was, San Antonio, Texas, to Fort Lauderdale, Florida, on to San Juan, Puerto Rico, then Trinidad and Tobago, ending with an overnight stay at the "upside down" Hilton Hotel, so named having been constructed on a cliff where the elevators went down to the guest rooms from the upper lobby. Next day, the flight plan originated in Trinidad and Tobago, then to Belem, Brazil, on to our final destination in Belo Horizonte, Brazil.

Belem was our port of entry for Brazilian customs and where we ran into problems when the agents wanted proof of insurance. It turned out we didn't have the required insurance documents. A local pilot observed our dilemma and suggested I should go to our plane on the pretext of looking for the document. There he joined me and said, "Show them anything!" Those custom "stupidos" won't know the difference.

On the blank back of the aircraft airworthy certificate, an official-looking document, I hand printed, "This aircraft insured by USAIG Insurance Company of Hartford Connecticut in the amount of "one million dollars US," and then I forged the signature of former President James Madison as current president of the insurance company. I considered signing George Washington, but that would have been pressing my luck a little too far. They probably weren't that "stupido."

I presented the certificate to the custom agent and he was all smiles and applied the numerous official stamps, and we were on our way after chewing out my copilot for not bringing the insurance document in the first place. That really upset my copilot big time, as that was really my job, and I thought he might throw a punch my way until I told him what I had done. He was still chuckling an hour later. On reaching our final destination that day in Belo Horizonte, Brazil, we had a meeting with the Lider Taxi Aereo, the largest operator of Learjets in South America at the time.

Lider Taxi Aereo had arranged our demo schedule. We planned to negotiate a contract with Lider to be our South American distributor and installation center. Our first demo was to a local owner who had a lease back with Lider. Everything went fine until we were ready to exit the plane upon completion of the flight.

A cable in the cabin entrance door mechanism failed, rendering it inoperable. The only way to vacate the plane was through the emergency exit window hatch. I was the first out to seek help (not living up to the tradition that the captain remains on a sinking ship), as it was close to a 100 degree day with high humidity, and the cabin was already becoming unbearable. I returned in a few minutes to discover our customer, who had a rather robust figure, could not fit through the emergency exit.

I heard swearing in Portuguese, something that I am certain was not complimentary. I re-entered the plane the same way I came out and started one engine in order to run the cabin air conditioner. If I hadn't, our now very unhappy customer would certainly have suffered heat stroke. He was still stuck in the cabin an hour later, the time needed to make repairs. I stood at the door to shake his hand and convey my apologies. I only received an unfriendly glance and a statement in Portuguese probably best not translated. Not a great way to start off our South American tour.

We did additional demos in São Paulo, a rather uninteresting and shabby city. Our longest stop was in Rio de

Janeiro. We demoed from Santos Dumont Airport, named after Alberto Santos Dumont. Santos Dumont (1873–1932) was an heir of a wealthy family of coffee producers.

Santos Dumont was an aviation pioneer and the father of Brazilian aviation. He spent most of his life in France and flew the first dirigible around the Eiffel Tower in 1901, making him very famous in Europe. He later designed, built, and flew several partially successful early flying machines. Some South American aviation historians claim he should have been credited with achieving the first controlled flight in a powered aircraft. This claim comes from the fact that Santos Dumont's design gained flight by using wheels for takeoff, whereas the Wright Brothers had to utilize a catapult to become airborne.

Santos Dumont returned to Brazil after being diagnosed with multiple sclerosis. Santos Dumont was also suffering from depression, and as a result of his failing health, he committed suicide by hanging.

Flying out of Santos Dumont airport, located on the Bay of Guanabara near downtown Rio, afforded some interesting sights during our demonstrations. The landing pattern brought you right around famous Sugar Loaf Mountain for a gorgeous birds-eye view.

As spectacular as our flights over Rio were, our stay at a Copacapana Beach Hotel was a great disappointment. The grand inlaid tile walkways seen in all the travel brochures were being used for automobile parking and were covered with grease and oil. The first item on my to-do list was to swim in the ocean and ogle the string bikini-clad Brazilian ladies struting their stuff up and down the beach. I arrived to find signs posted "NO SWIMMING ALLOWED; OCEAN

POLLUTED" The ladies must have had advance warning. They were a definite no show.

Our thrust reverser demonstration tour in Brazil resulted in Lider making several sales and installations. Our next stop was in Buenos Aires, Argentina, where two demos were scheduled. These ended up no shows. To this day, I never figured out what we did to offend our Argentine clients. Maybe they found out I didn't like Andrew Lloyd Webber's musical *Evita*.

After that frustrating visit to Argentina, we departed for Lima, Peru, with a fuel stop in La Paz, Bolivia, which was at that time the world's highest airport at an elevation of 13,323 feet. Years later, the Chinese built an airport in Bangda, Tibet, that sits at an elevation of 14,219 feet, making it now the world's highest airport. After fueling and a potty break, our old reliable GE engines wouldn't start, due to the extremely thin air density. Luckily, a GE engine field technician accompanied us on the tour and knew how to remedy the problem.

Both engines had to be uncowled, in order to increase fuel density in the fuel controllers, hopefully correcting the starting problem. We had to sit down and catch our breath about every five minutes. The locals, used to that altitude, were surely laughing behind our backs.

The engines finally started with the help of a borrowed Braniff Airlines battery cart, as our aircraft batteries were depleted from the unsuccessful engine starts. Normally, when you advanced the throttles on a Learjet for takeoff, the engines have a distinctive powerful sound and the acceleration presses you back in your seat. On the takeoff from La Paz, the engines barely let out a hum, and the acceleration was excruciatingly slow. Our friends in Brazil warned us that several Learjets had blown their tires on takeoff from La Paz by keeping the plane on the runway too long trying to achieve safe single engine flying speed (a.k.a. V1) and actually exceeded the tires maximum certified speed of 200 knots. This experience resulted in an interesting education on jet airplane high altitude performance.

Our next destination on the tour was Lima, Peru. This route would take us over the heart of the Andes Mountains. We looked forward to some spectacular views from our cruising altitude of 41,000 feet. No views on this flight. The Andes were completely obscured with a long line of large and violent thunderstorms. We flew parallel to the line of storms, searching with our airborne weather radar for a safe way through. About the time I was ready to turn back, with fuel reserves becoming an issue, a small gap between storm cells appeared on the radar screen. But we did experience heavy rain and moderate turbulence for a short time.

These types of encounters with severe weather always resulted in a rise in "pucker factor" for those in the cockpit. I underwent many more similar moments than I care to remember during my 62 years of defying gravity.

Our weather deviation took us about 200 miles south of our intended route. Radar coverage was very limited in South America. Only major airports provided radar service with a limited range of 100 miles. Our deviation had taken us out of Lima's radar coverage. They knew our estimated time of arrival (ETA) from our flight plan and requested a position report. We reported 200 miles south, at best an educated guess, with no navigation aids to work with. Global Positioning System (GPS) was years away from development.

GPS is now the primary navigation system for aircraft. Any pilot today with a GPS-equipped airplane that gets lost should stick to water sports.

We turned back north toward Lima and had some nice views of the Peruvian coastline. Radar contact was reestablished, and approach and landing at Lima were routine. While cruising at an altitude of 41,000 feet with relatively no chance of encountering other aircraft, we enjoyed the serenity that can only come from flight.

No airliners of the day had the capability to fly that high, and the military operated in restricted airspace. We were simply cruising in a Learjet kind of world. On landing, we discovered the city of Lima was under martial law. "The Shining Path," a Maoist guerilla insurgent group operating in Peru, had fire bombed the Hilton hotel, where we held reservations. There were soldiers armed with submachine guns on every downtown street corner. Enjoying breakfast the next morning proved somewhat difficult. About the time our eggs were being served, a soldier walked up, stood, and stared at us through the restaurant window. He had a hungry look in his eye, and the barrel of his weapon kept pointing in our direction. I started wondering how well the Peruvian Army screened their recruits for terrorist leanings. As I tried to swallow my eggs, I began feeling like a sitting duck in a carnival shooting gallery.

The next day we received clearance to the local military airport. The Peruvian Air Force had purchased four Learjets and equipped them for high altitude photography. On arrival, we were escorted to the commanding general's office. The general's grandparents were from England, and he spoke excellent English with a sometimes difficult Cockney accent. After formalities, he reached into his desk drawer and presented what appeared to be a tube of lipstick. When he twisted the knob, a small erect penis popped out. The general thought this hilarious and looked for our approval. We were there to sell thrust reversers, so I never laughed so hard in my life. Each of us left Lima with a present of our very own "pop-out penis." I actually looked for mine recently and, like many of life's little treasures, it has somehow quietly disappeared!

At this point, I was wondering what could possibly top this. That answer arrived a short time later as the general presented himself for the demo decked out in a flame-red flight suit with flying gloves, (fingers cut off at the first knuckle), not that he was ever going to touch the controls. His outfit was topped off with a general service hat, complete with gold scrambled egg adornment. He appeared appropriately dressed for a guest appearance on *Hogan's Heroes*, the popular TV show that somewhat ridiculed the military.

I performed my usual demo and observed he had his mind elsewhere. We were headed back for our final landing when he pointed out a mountain ridge in the distance and asked if we could fly over there. After clearing the ridge, we came out over a lovely valley with a very affluent looking community. He then pointed out a particular house and asked if we could fly over it at a low altitude (commonly referred to as a "buzz job"). On the first pass, a young lady appeared waving with much enthusiasm. He asked for another pass, so I actually completed three passes, dropping lower each time. By this time, our general was almost beside himself with joy and explained that the young damsel, hardly in distress, was in fact his "amante" or, in other words, his mistress.

I will always remember this experience as a romantic

respite from an otherwise routine commercial experience, as our language falls well short of capturing the emotions of the moment. Rather than the "Mistress Demo," I have filed the experience away in Spanish as the "amante de la demostración."

The next day was scheduled for a demo to Peruvian Learjet captains. The day's flight turned into an actual emergency. During one of the landing gear retractions, a hydraulic hose failed and we lost all hydraulic pressure. The emergency landing gear extension system was activated, and the landing gear extended and locked in the down position. The emergency brake system was operated by a standby air bottle and was difficult to operate without damaging the plane's tires.

One of the main safety features of the Dee Howard Thrust Reverser System was a backup hydraulic accumulator. With a total hydraulic failure, the accumulator retained enough pressure to deploy and stow the thrust reverser. After landing, the reversers deployed as advertised, and a minimal amount of emergency braking was used to bring the aircraft to a safe stop.

The captains were very impressed with the system, and I thought for sure that a sale would ensue. The sale never occurred. Perhaps the general was focusing on flyovers and mistress rendezvous rather than equipping his fleet of Learjets with our thrust reversers.

A new hydraulic line was crafted at the Peruvian Air Force maintenance shop. The next task was to service the hydraulic system with new fluid. The hydraulic reservoir in a Learjet was located in the aft fuselage with an access door located in the belly of the plane. This area was commonly known as the "hell hole" due to its very tight quarters. The hydraulic tank was almost inaccessible and could only be reasonably serviced with a hydraulic pressure tank. The Peruvians did not have one. I watched with interest as a mechanic approached the hell hole with a can of hydraulic fluid and a funnel. He was wearing sparkling white overalls. When standing in the hell hole, only his waist to his feet was visible.

From experience, I knew what was coming! Muffled Spanish swear words echoed out of the hell hole, and it was not long before streams of bright red hydraulic fluid began to flow down the pant legs of his once pristine white overalls. By the time he was finished, he was completely bathed in the red fluid with two large puddles surrounding his feet. Much to his credit, the poor fellow did manage to properly service the hydraulic reservoir.

After weeks on the road, we were tired and ready to head home. Guayaquil, Ecuador, and Managua, Nicaragua, were our last two fuel stops on the way home. We arrived at Guayaquil about four p.m. on a Friday afternoon. We knew that the Ecuadorian Air Force had purchased two new Model 24 Learjets, but they had not yet been delivered to this rapidly developing South American nation. On final approach, there sat two brand new Learjets shining in the afternoon sunlight. Obviously our information was out of date, and perhaps a chance for a final unscheduled demonstration was still in order. I didn't think there was much of a chance finding anyone in the military at the airport late on a Friday afternoon. I instructed my copilot to fuel our plane, and I would take a chance by inquiring around the terminal. In the terminal I found a lady who spoke English, and I asked if she knew who was in charge of the Learjets parked outside.

She knew the man in charge was a Major Garcia. I further asked if he might be contacted. In an amazing short time, I had spoken to Major Garcia who, in turn, had spoken to his commanding officer, and a demonstration was scheduled for the following morning. I rushed back to stop the fueling, but too late. We had a full load of jet fuel. The rather obsolete fuel truck did not have the capability to defuel. The major arrived about this time, and I explained we could not demonstrate the thrust reversers with a full load of fuel.

Our only alternative was to fly around the area and burn off enough fuel to arrive at safe landing weights. He understood and said he would love to be my copilot and take care of the flight planning. I asked if we needed to file an official form with the airport authorities. He assured me he could do it by radio with the control tower. All his radio transmissions were in rapid Spanish. He gave me a "thumbs up" and off we went. We never climbed higher than 500 feet of altitude in order to burn off the excess fuel in the shortest amount of time.

To the major's delight we buzzed his uncle's banana plantation and numerous cargo ships sailing to the port up the Guayas River. In about 30 minutes, we had consumed enough fuel and returned for landing. On engine shut down in our parking spot, we were greeted by two soldiers with automatic weapons. The major informed me we were to report to the airport Comandante muy pronto.

The airport Comandante was an air force colonel, and upon entering his office, he burst out with a tirade that I had made an unauthorized flight, my airplane would be impounded, and I was going straight to jail! I hit a brace like the old aviation cadet days and tried to explain that the major had arranged the flight plan. He grew more angry and stated that here the major had no authority. With that outburst, the major made a quick exit, and I was alone to defend myself.

I remained in the stiffest brace possible and continued to plead my case. At one time, I thought he might strike me, he was so overwrought. He finally calmed down somewhat and sat down at his desk. I should have called it a day, but being a salesman to the last, I mentioned our thrust reverser demonstration scheduled for the following morning.

You would have thought a red hot poker had been inserted through the bottom of his chair. He jumped up and stood in my face with a finger pointed inches from my nose and said, "Americano, you only have permission to leave now!" This time I took his advice without hesitation and made a not-too-graceful exit.

Since it was now late in the evening, we were given permission to stay overnight. The only good thing to come out of this chaotic stop was that I stayed in the nicest hotel and had the best dinner of the entire South American trip. After an uneventful fuel stop in Managua, we safely returned home with my experience in Ecuador etched forever in my memory. How good it felt to be back on good old United States soil, more convinced than ever I was blessed to live in the grandest country in the world.

Chapter Nine
Odds and Ends and a Should Have Been

In the mid1970s time frame, during one of my weekends in Germany, I was invited to the town carnival. It had all the normal rides and games just like our carnivals in the USA. I came across a "Schützenfest" (German, for a "shooting gallery"). The gallery was equipped with air-powered pellet rifles and moving targets. I was at the prime time of my life and was an excellent marksman. I shot in sequence two complete rifle loads of pellets (30 rounds) and never missed one of the moving rabbits or ducks as they came into view.

The attendant, who was the owner of the gallery, handed me my prize and asked, "You American man?" I responded, "You bet, sir." With an expression on his face that I could not determine was of admiration or dislike toward me, he said with a heavy German accent, "No vunder ve lost der var."

The Hannover, Germany, air show was a weeklong annual affair that attracted planes and vendors from all over the world. I was there with a copilot and our insurance agent, and it became our habit to eat in our hotel every evening. This process became very boring by the end of the week. I asked a German pilot friend attending the air show if he could suggest a typical small German village where we could experience genuine German country fare. He suggested a village about a one-hour drive from Hannover. The village was everything we had imagined. Houses were built with thatched roofs on cobbled streets consistent with architecture of the previous century. The restaurant we visited was small, but charming, and the wait staff did not speak English. So, the ordering of the meal was almost a game of charades as it was necessary to gesture with our hands in order to make our selections. The meal was excellent, and as we were ready to pay and leave, four big German local men entered the restaurant and took seats at the bar. They seemed to take notice of the "foreigners" in the restaurant, and it was very noticeable that they did not appreciate our presence.

As I paid our bill, a round of Schnapps was delivered to our table, compliments of the men at the bar. I thought it would be a good idea to toast our new friends as the second round of drinks appeared at our table. The rounds continued to come, and I then determined that enough was enough, and that we were near the point of intoxication.

So, we elected to leave while we still could under our own power, and the largest of the four gentlemen blocked our path and said, "You Englishman?" I told him no, that we were Americans. He then demanded to see our passports. Due to his size and unfriendly demeanor, I complied with his request. Once he was satisfied that we were indeed Americans, he moved aside, and while still glaring at us, said "gute nacht" which was German for *goodnight*.

We left the village wondering what was behind the unfriendly welcome by the four locals. The following day we asked the German pilot, who had recommended the venue to us, what was their issue with the English? He explained to me that area of Germany had suffered through relentless nighttime fire-bombing by the Royal Air Force (RAF) during World War II on a daily basis. The Americans, though certainly not well liked either, were held in a higher esteem as they had restricted their bombing runs to daylight hours where their risk of being shot down was much higher.

The consensus among us was that our restaurant friends planned to get us drunk and then escort us outside where they could take their revenge by treating us to a good thrashing. We made it a point not to wander into the German countryside again without being accompanied by a German companion. It was difficult for me to believe this type of anger still existed 31 years after the end of WWII.

Another nonflying adventure experienced in Germany in the early 1980s involved delivering a German customer model 35 Learjet to Hannover. After the delivery, I needed to also travel to Kiel to visit with a potential customer. Kiel is the far northern German seaport on the Baltic Sea, famous for the bomb-proof U-Boat submarine pens built during WWII. There was no direct airline service, so for the first time, I opted to travel by railroad. I made the novice mistake of purchasing a second-class ticket. The four-hour trip was a bit unusual to say the least. I was joined by farmers with a hodgepodge of chickens, ducks, and other farm animals, bringing a mixture of overwhelming odors. I made sure of a shower and change of clothes before my meeting.

I planned an upgrade to first class for my return trip. Unfortunately the ticket agent at the Kiel train station ("Bahnhof" in German) did not speak enough English, nor I enough German, to get my upgrade request understood.

The train started to pull out exactly on time, as all German trains do. One thing I had learned was the number one painted on the side of the car meant first class. A number one car passed in front of me and I noticed it had no passengers, so I jumped on board. I stored my luggage, removed my jacket and tie, and selected a comfortable seat, anticipating a peaceful ride back to Hannover. In about 15 minutes, the conductor entered the car and asked for my ticket. He said in German, "Sir, you are in first class with a second class ticket." I gave him my best "I don't understand/ completely befuddled" look. He repeated the same in almost perfect English. I appeared even more befuddled. I now made a calculated risk that the conductor might be bilingual, but I bet he didn't speak a word of Spanish.

I stood up as if alarmed and said, "Problema señor? Que paso? Soy de España and a few other Spanish words thrown in for good luck. I could tell immediately he figured this was just not worth pursuing. He muttered a few German words, which luckily I didn't understand, and punched my ticket. I shook his hand and with a broad smile said, "Muchas gracias, señor; hasta la vista."

I met Herr Uwe H. Fischer at the 1976 Hannover Air Show in Germany, where I demonstrated the Dee Howard MKII thrust reverser-equipped Learjet. This encounter turned into a lifetime friendship, plus a successful business association. Uwe was a post-WWII Luftwaffe pilot, and he was a pioneer in developing private aviation in Germany after the war. He was also president of the German Kennel Club, an international dog show judge, and an avid hunter. He was invited to judge behind the Iron Curtain in countries like Poland, Hungary, and other Warsaw Pact Nations. There he met dog owners who shared his hunting aspirations.

Arrangements were made by his new friends for him to hunt in their countries still under Russian rule. After several years of establishing himself with these hunters, he inquired if he might bring an American friend. So my hunting behind the Iron Curtain came to pass.

The one hunt I shall never forget took place in Poland. The hunts were much regulated, with a specific area assigned to each hunting party, and were always accompanied by a professional guide. One morning we were assigned our area for the day, and just after breakfast were told our guide had called in ill. Uwe, who was a very determined man, convinced the hunting master that he had hunted there many times before and knew the area well enough that we could safely hunt alone. To my amazement, the permission was granted, a very rare event indeed.

Our hunting vehicle was a bright red CJ-7 Jeep Uwe had purchased on one of his visits to San Antonio. While there, the CJ-7 had the latest state-of-the-art stereo system installed. I drove it to Houston and shipped the Jeep to Germany by ship to Bremerhaven. It was his pride and joy to show off in "Comrade Land." We were informed that the normal road to our hunting area was barricaded, and we were verboten to use it, with no real explanation why. We had to take a detour to reach our hunting area, which added about 40 kilometers to our drive.

We hunted to almost dark, and upon our return drive, the barricade that was previously up on the other end of our forbidden road was down. I was for taking the detour home, but Herr Fisher didn't want to miss cocktail hour at the hunting lodge. The roads we traveled were narrow dirt logging trails with thick evergreen trees growing right up to the road's edge. As we drove on in the growing dusk, I began to notice objects protruding from the trees that no longer resembled branches. THEY WERE TANK CANNON BARRELS!

We were driving through the middle of a camouflaged Russian tank squadron. Soldiers came running out of the woods, and I asked Uwe, "What in the hell are we going to do now?" He remembered I had attended a Russian language course in the military and said, "Holler something in Russian!" He cranked up the stereo full volume, not playing Russian patriotic songs, but American rock and roll, and floored the accelerator.

All I could remember in that moment of panic was the Russian word for good or fine, "Xopowo" (pronounced Ha-ra-sho). I hollered Ha-ra-sho so many times it must still be echoing throughout that forest. We drove around the other barricade through the woods and arrived back at the hunting lodge in the dark. We dared not tell our Polish friends what happened. Instead we had a stiff drink of vodka and hunkered down, waiting for the Russian hammer and sickle to descend upon us. To our amazement, not a word or inquiry was ever heard.

If that Russian tank commander is alive and telling this same story to friends over drinks of vodka, I can only imagine he is still saying, "Who in the hell were those two guys in that red Jeep playing rock and roll music and hollering Ha-ra-sho?"

Two weeks before Christmas 1988, I was asked by one of my best German customers to fly his Learjet Model 36 from Munich to Tucson for major work, including new paint and a refurbished interior. The model 36 was the long-range version of 30 series Learjets.

It carried 210 gallons more fuel, giving it a nonstop range of 2,500 nautical miles (2,875 statute miles). This extra range made the North Atlantic crossing much easier with fewer fuel stops. Our first leg was from Munich to Keflavik, Iceland, the second leg was Keflavik to Winnipeg, Canada, with the last leg to our final destination in Tucson, Arizona.

We encountered stronger than forecast headwinds about halfway between Iceland and Winnipeg. It was determined that we could not fly the leg nonstop. An alternate airport was needed. Churchill, Manitoba, is a small community on top of Hudson Bay and known as the polar bear capital of the world. It lay directly ahead on our route. The airport was a former USAF base during the Cold War, and fuel and most landing facilities were still available. We could not have asked for a better alternate landing spot.

In late December, Northern Canada is covered in deep snow. We taxied into the parking area with snow piled up on all sides, eight feet high, and with a temperature of minus 25 degrees. We did not have clothing for these conditions and nearly froze to death trying to service the airplane. We were just about ready to depart when a snowmobile pulled up with a driver covered in a heavy artic parka. He asked who was in charge of the plane, and as he removed his parka, the uniform of a Royal Canadian Policeman appeared.

At this point of the story, I must explain that I was in command of a German-registered airplane with a German copilot, and the owner's chief mechanic and his wife were on board as passengers. The Mountie asked, "Captain, where did you come from and where are you going?" My response was, "Sir, we came from Iceland, and our destination is Tucson, Arizona."

That answer seemed to stun him a bit, and then he asked, "And where did you clear Canadian customs? Churchill is not a port of entry." It was my turn to be stunned, as with all the headwind problems and fuel reserve worries, clearing customs had slipped my mind.

I carefully explained our fuel situation and our reason for landing at his airport. I could see the wheels going around in his head, contemplating all the forms to fill out, confiscating the Learjet, and making arrangements for four foreigners to be locked up in town.

He thought for a few minutes and said, "I suppose you lads would like to be getting home for Christmas? I am going to pretend you were never here. You have permission to leave. Please come back someday and see all our polar bears, but not without officially clearing Canadian customs first."

I hope that the Mountie had a wonderful life. He saved me a long explanation to my German customer that his airplane was being confiscated, and to my wife as to why I would be spending Christmas and an unknown amount of time with polar bears in Churchill, Canada!

Can you imagine that scenario playing out in our present world of terrorism and tight security? By the way, we overflew the city of Winnipeg and exited Canadian airspace without ever officially clearing customs. Shame on me!

Long distance flying without the proper equipment can be challenging. In another North Atlantic crossing, I returned home with an early model 25 Learjet taken in trade with the sale of a model 35 to one of my German customers. The shorter range Learjet 25 would again require numerous fuel stops. We departed Berlin, to Bergen, Norway, to Keflavik, Iceland, to Frobisher Bay, Canada (now named Iqaluit), to Thunder Bay, Ontario, and the final leg to Tucson.

In the 1980s and early nineties, the long-range navigation system of the time was Global Navigation System (GNS).

GNS fixed an aircraft's position by triangulation of three ground stations. The GNS was fairly accurate, but nowhere as accurate as our modern GPS technology. Our Model 25 Learjet was not equipped with GNS, so arrangements were made in Germany to have a portable unit installed. This unit failed about two hours into our flight. It was not likely anyone at our stops had the capability to repair the unit, and returning to Berlin was not a good option. So the decision to forge on without long-range navigation information was made.

The flight progressed routinely until our leg between Iceland and Frobisher Bay. This route took us over the top of Greenland where we received an amendment to our flight plan. The new air traffic control clearance included a waypoint, which could only be found on our broken GNS. Fortunately, from the information on our aeronautical charts, the new waypoint was located at the end of a very distinguished fjord on the West Coast of Greenland. Our Collins AVQ 21 weather radar had great ground mapping capabilities.

We flew west on a heading we hoped would be fairly accurate, and soon our fjord appeared on the radar screen. I guessed we were as close to the waypoint as we were going to get, and I picked up the mic to make a position report.

Before I could key the mic, Alitalia flight 460 reported over the waypoint at flight level 370 (37,000 feet). That was 6,000 feet below our flight level of 410 (41,000 feet). I looked down and an Alitalia Boeing 747 passed right under us. We were not in the vicinity of the waypoint—we were right over it!

The chances of anyone duplicating that navigation feat

are slim to none. No one today could fake their way across the North Atlantic without an operable long-range navigation system as we did. Modern air traffic control technology would make it impossible. The days of improvising, flying by the seat of your pants, and the pure romance of flying are slowly but surely being lost in today's high-tech environment. I truly miss them.

Learjet registration number N111JD, serial number 23-006, was the sixth airplane to be manufactured by the new Learjet Company in Wichita, Kansas. Bill Lear originally had plans to single pilot certify the Learjet line. The first nine Model 23s built had all the system controls installed on the pilot's side, or left side, of the cockpit. They were nicknamed "the left hand drive Lear." Single pilot certification was never approved, and all Learjets required a crew of two.

Left hand drive N111JD was originally owned by the John Deere Company and was referred to by the phrase "Triple One JD" in order to shorten radio transmits. She had been sitting in the corner of a hangar in Fort Wayne, Indiana, collecting dust for over a year. The airplane was being offered at a very attractive price and was a perfect candidate for resale, upgraded with the Howard thrust reversers and MKII systems installed. A sales deal was made, and the seller agreed to provide a copilot for the delivery flight to San Antonio.

I spent several days with a local mechanic checking all airframe and engine systems to determine if the plane was airworthy for the delivery flight. Late on day two, I informed the seller we were ready to depart and to supply my copilot. A young man showed up, and after introductions, I inquired how much Learjet time he had logged. He replied, "None, sir." He did hold instrument and multi-engine ratings. The most complex aircraft he was qualified in was a Cessna 310, a twin engine, piston powered airplane. With all the controls on my side, he needed only work the radios with air traffic control (ATC). So I made the decision to depart later in the day than I would have preferred, due to afternoon thunderstorms in the forecast. I gave my new partner a short briefing on emergency procedures and our takeoff was routine.

We climbed to our cruising altitude of 41,000 feet. Approaching Evansville, Indiana, we encountered a large line of developing thunderstorms. With the help of our weather radar, we were picking our way through the soft spots when the radar screen went blank. System Failure Number One! A short time later, I felt my ears pop and noticed the cabin altitude rising rapidly. I operated the emergency pressurization controls with no results. The cabin altitude had already risen to a danger level of 15,000 feet. System Failure Number Two!

The thought that bad things always happen in "threes" passed through my mind. Should I trust the standby oxygen system that I had not checked that well? As much as I dreaded letting down into the tempest beneath us, I made the decision an emergency descent was clearly the safest maneuver to prevent the likelihood of becoming incapacitated.

I ordered my young copilot to don his mask. The poor boy had no idea what was taking place. I made a rapid radio call to ATC that we were having pressurization problems and were executing an emergency descent now! I entered the top of the storm, and the ride was violent. We encountered severe turbulence, heavy rain, and frequent clattering of hail against the plane. My radio call to ATC was most likely too rapid in the excitement of the moment, and they kept calling, "Triple

One JD, say again," over and over. I was much too busy trying to save the plane and our lives to respond.

We briefly came out in the clear between storm cells, and I again told ATC we were in an emergency descent. The only response was a repeat of "Triple One JD, say again." During all this mayhem, another jet on our same frequency made an open radio call that, to the best of my memory, went something like this: "ATC, why not give those poor guys in Triple One JD a break and let them try to solve their problems?!"

After what seemed an eternity, but, in fact, was a matter of minutes, we broke out of the weather at 10,000 feet and, for reasons unknown, the pressurization system started functioning again. I was able to remove my mask and, with a much calmer voice, advised ATC that our situation was under control.

I had been much too busy to concern myself with my inexperienced Learjet copilot. I looked his way for the first time since I told him to don his mask. The poor soul was white as a sheet, with eyes as big as saucers, and was breathing so hard I was afraid he might ingest his mask. I told him things were now under control, it was safe to remove the mask, and we would continue on to San Antonio at a lower cruising altitude in case the pressurization system acted up again.

He did not respond and without any expression stared straight ahead. After a few minutes, he asked me, "Did you hear that voice on the radio talking to ATC?"

I answered, "What voice?"

"The one telling ATC to leave us alone!"

I said I vaguely remember something like that. He then

put a trembling hand on my shoulder and said in a whispering voice, **"That was God talking to us."** I doubt my young copilot would be very anxious to ever be a crew member in another Learjet any time soon. Needless to say, I was not too pleased with the whole episode myself. Surely my heart rate was, most likely, off the charts for a while. Many hundreds of hours of Learjet flying time still lay ahead of me on my way west.

For one of my early corporate flying jobs in the 1960s, long before my Learjet days, I was piloting an Aero Commander model 680 for a real estate developer in Chicago. The 680 was a piston-powered, high-wing, six-passenger twin engine airplane that was quite popular during that era.

My boss was good friends with Mr. Oster of Osterizer blender fame. Mr. Oster purchased a special breed of mountain dog on a visit to Germany. He made arrangements to have it delivered via air to Chicago's O'Hare Airport. My job was to pick up the dog at the Lufthansa air freight office and fly him to Milwaukee, Mr. Oster's hometown. I was told the dog was just a puppy, and I envisioned a fairly small animal. My boss suggested it would be a good idea to buy a box of dog biscuits to make friends with my passenger. On arrival at the freight office, I was introduced to a puppy that already weighed close to a hundred pounds. I mentally named him Rex (Latin for "king").

His dog carrier was too large to fit through the door of the 680, so I tied Rex to a rear seat of the cabin by his leash. Rex was calm and collected until we lifted into the air on takeoff. He became frantic and broke loose of the leash. He came bounding up to the cockpit and pushed his large paws into the middle of the throttle quadrant (engine controls). The 680 was not equipped with an autopilot.

#17 AERO COMMANDER 680

The weight of Rex moving from the rear to the front of the cabin required me to immediately manually trim the plane to keep the center of gravity (CG) within limits. I was overwhelmed with the CG problem and trying, among the paws, to manipulate the engine controls in order to keep us from returning to what we had just departed, the unforgiving ground.

Luckily, I had placed the box of dog biscuits on the copilot's seat where I could grab one and toss it to the back of the cabin. Rex would consume the biscuit and come bounding back into the cockpit. Re-trim, reset the engine controls, and throw another biscuit! This scenario repeated itself for the entire flight. Thankfully the trip was only 40 minutes, or, a more apt description, two dozen doggie treats long, for I was down to my last dog biscuit on our final approach to landing. I never saw Rex again. I hope he made Mr. Oster a great companion. I am sure he consumed huge amounts of dog biscuits when he was fully grown.

Chapter Ten
The Golden Years

On one of my last jet flights from Bangor, Maine, to Keflavik, Iceland, at night, en route to Germany in a Learjet model 55, cruising at an attitude of 45,000 feet the aurora borealis, the Northern Lights remained in view for hours off the left wing of the plane. It appeared like a waterfall in a never-ending cascade of light in hues of silver, blue, and green, truly an awesome sight. We had no camera on board to record this fantastic phenomenon.

#18 MY LAST DELIVERY OF A LEARJET MODEL 55
GERMAN REGISTRATION NO. D-CREW

As my copilot and I were completing our descent checklist on our approach to Iceland, he leaned toward me and said, "Al, we have seen and done things in our lifetimes that most people only dream about." I have so many memories to take with me into my Golden Years.

Shortly after retiring, I joined Angel Flight, a nonprofit, nationwide organization of pilots who volunteer their planes to provide transportation for patients who could not afford the expense of trips for treatment to medical facilities faraway. One of my frequent patients was Judy, a lady suffering from advanced breast cancer, who lived in Alamogordo, New Mexico. She was being treated at the MD Anderson Cancer Institute in Houston, Texas, a distance of 800 miles.

Angel Flight would break up the trip into three equal legs. My leg was Alamogordo to Midland, Texas, a flight of one hour and 15 minutes in my Beechcraft Bonanza. Another Angel Pilot would fly the next leg from Midland to the Austin, Texas, area, and the third on to Houston. The return trip was achieved in reverse order. I made this trip with Judy several times.

Judy's sister, Tresa, would always accompany us on the return trip, as Judy was weak and in need of some assistance after a week of radiation and chemo treatments. Tresa always sat in the seats in the back of the cabin, and Judy liked to occupy the copilot seat next to me.

On one of our return trips from Midland, Texas, back to Alamogordo, New Mexico, Tresa was studying material she needed in order to renew her nursing certificate. She told me that as she reviewed the material, a thought had crossed her mind. She jotted it down and returned to her material. As we flew, her thoughts continued to interrupt her studies, and by the time we landed, she had composed her very first poem. She felt that, without a doubt, the verses came from God.

Safe Within Their Fold
Tresa Van Winkle

It is amazing how an illness can deplete you through the years
The loss of fun and function, treatment worries, money fears.
At times the thought of travel to the doctor far away
Is more than one can handle when they've barely made the day
But the light of hope is brightened when an Angel phones to say
"I'll pick you up and fly you . . ." to the doctor on this day.
Now these are mighty Angels, you feel safe within their fold
For their wings are forged in metal and their hearts the purest gold.
Your faith in mankind broadens as you travel through the sky
And you look into the Angel's eyes and simply wonder . . . why?
They donate time and talent to care for you today
Then view their acts of charity, as simply "Angel Play"!
You know God has anointed them to help you win your fight . . .
Mighty Angels dressed as humans form the ranks of
"ANGEL FLIGHT"!

Judy left us to be with the Lord a few months after the poem was written. I still have fond memories flying across the country with Judy at my side chatting, and to her delight, pointing out interesting landmarks along the way. After all the years, I still cannot read the poem without suppressing a tear as I approach the last verse. With all the ups and downs one experiences in a lifetime, my five years serving as an Angel Flight pilot were some of the most rewarding of my life.

It's hard to realize I've been retired for 15 years and

residing in the beautiful pine- and aspen-covered mountains of southeastern New Mexico. A home, sitting at a height of 7,000 feet is almost like flying. We have ideal weather all year round. In some winter months, one can ski in the morning and play golf in the afternoon. I treasure each hour of every day, giving thanks to God for granting me a second life, which hopefully, in his eyes, I have fulfilled.

I am still privileged to own a Beechcraft Bonanza airplane, which I fly and maintain with tender loving care. I know as I approach my 80th year, this will be my last flying machine in a long line of 111 different types of airplanes and helicopters I have flown throughout my career.

Many people have asked me over the years, "Of all the different airplanes you have flown, which one is your favorite?" My response: "They were all my favorites." Each one had its own set of performance and flight characteristics. Some were docile and forgiving; others had unpredictable traits that could trap the unwary pilot. No matter what plane I was piloting, as soon as the wheels lifted off the ground, I felt the exhilaration of flight. With confidence and being in command, the controls ever responding to my slightest touch, I guided my willing craft upward into the vivid blue above, never anxious to return to the sullen bonds of earth.

From donating blood to make ends meet in the early days, to flying jet airplanes around the world, to rubbing elbows with famous celebrities and world leaders, to hunting behind the Iron Curtain, to my miraculous survival in the ocean—it has been one hell of a ride! I am again reminded of that remark from my fellow aviator as we were descending for landing in Iceland that night years ago, "Al, we have seen and done things in our life times that most people only dream about."

"He has gone west," a phrase used by aviators when a fellow pilot passes away, "not alone into the sunset, but into the company of friends who have gone before." I am sure somewhere on down the road when two pilots are planning the day's flight over a cup of morning coffee, one might say, "By the way, did you hear that ol' Al Ackerman has gone west?"

THE END

This book would never have been written without the love, support, and inspiration of my wife, Deborah.

Notable Persons I Encountered on "My Journey West"

(Note: not all are mentioned in the book)

Politicians:

Lyndon Baines Johnson   38th president of the United States of America

Hubert H. Humphrey   38th vice president of the United States of America

Jim Wright   Speaker of the house of representatives 1987–1989 and the only speaker ever to resign due to ethics violations

Edwin Muskie   US senator from Maine and democratic nominee for president in 1972

Dolph Briscoe   Governor of Texas 1973–1979

Entertainers:

Minnie Pearl   of Grand Ole Opry fame

Betty Hutton   Movie actress, singer, and comedienne of the 1940s and 50's

Frank Sinatra   Chairman of the Board

Danny Kaye	Movie actor, singer, and comedian from 1930 to 1980
Steppenwolf	Rock group of the 1960s and '70s
Conway Twitty	Country and western music star of the 1970s and '80s
Hank Williams Jr.	Country and western star 1960s to present
The Osmond Brothers	Singing group 1950s to present

Sports:

A.J. Foyt	Acclaimed race driver who won four Indy 500 car races 1960's and '70s and still has his own race team
Illi Nastase	Romanian tennis great, winner of seven Grand Slam titles, and remembered for his flamboyant on court antics
Bobby Allison	Won 84 races in NASCAR's top division, including three Daytona 500 events and named among top 50 all-time greatest drivers
John Brodie	Star quarterback of the Stanford Cardinal and San Francisco 49ers football teams and also named MVP of the 1970 season

Aviation:

Eddie Rickenbacker	Race driver, WWI ace, and leader of the famous 94th Aero (Hat in the Ring) Squadron; pioneer of commercial aviation and chairman of Eastern Air Lines 1890–1973
Roscoe Turner	Famous air racer won the Thompson Trophy three times; flew with a lion cub in the cockpit to promote his sponsor, Gilmore Oil, 1920s and '30s
David L. (Tex) Hill	Ace and leader of the American Volunteer Group (AVG) named the Flying Tigers 1940 to 1941.
Paul Tibbets	Pilot of the B29 bomber named Enola Gay that dropped the first atomic bomb on Hiroshima Japan 1945
Bill Lear	Inventor of many aviation radios and autopilots; developer of the Learjet; one of aviation's great entrepreneurs
Moya Lear	Wife of Bill Lear and daughter of Ole Olsen of the famous vaudeville act Olsen & Johnson 1920–1940; *Hellzapoppen* was their most popular Broadway show

Dee U. Howard	Aircraft designer and modifier held more Supplemental Type Certificates (FAA-approved modifications to production aircraft) than anyone in the industry
Ed Swearingen	Designer of many aircraft modifications and builder of the Merlin and Metroliner turbo props
Jim Raisbeck	Designer of the Howard Raisbeck MKII system and numerous performance improvements for the Beechcraft King Air class of turbo props
Clay Lacy	Pilot extraordinaire; holder of many speed and distance records; flight leader of Bill Lear's funeral flyover in Reno, Nevada
Chuck Yeager	WWII ace who flew 61 missions shot down over France and with the help of the Maquis (French resistance); escaped from a German Prisoner of War camp; first man to break the sound barrier in a rocket propelled Bell X-1 aircraft October 14, 1947; retired a brigadier general.

Business and Financiers:

Robert Vesco — Fugitive financier of the 1970s; fled to the Caribbean with an estimated 200 million dollars; died in a Cuban prison after serving 13 years in confinement for drug trafficking

Christina Onnasis — Daughter of Aristotle Onnasis and a Learjet owner

Dr. Forest Bird — Lifetime aviator and designer of innovative and lifesaving medical respirators and ventilators owner and pilot of a Howard 500

John Oster — Designer of the Osterizer and other home appliances

George Stephen — Designer of the Weber Kettle Grill and the Weber Company; owned and operated a Howard 250

W. Smucker — Grandson of Jerome Monroe Smucker, founder of the JM Smucker Company in Orrville, Ohio, 1897; "With a name like Smucker's, it has to be good"

Salem bin Laden — brother of Osama bin Laden; took over the family business empire in 1967 and owner of several Learjets; he was killed in an ultra-light aircraft accident in San Antonio, Texas, in 1988

CPSIA information can be obtained
at www.ICGtesting.com
Printed in the USA
FSOW03n1405081217
41725FS

9 781626 525344